I AM GRATEFUL TO GOD FOR EVERYTHING! AND FOR YOU, HAVE
CHOSE THIS COLORING BOOK. C.A, I'M GLAD TO
BE MAKING YOU HAVE FUN, THANK YOU VERY MUCH.
LOV U

SARAH ELISA

2024

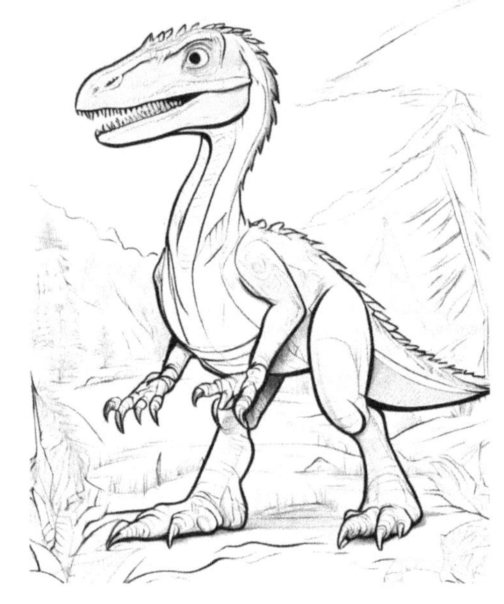

THIS BOOK BELONGS TO:

____

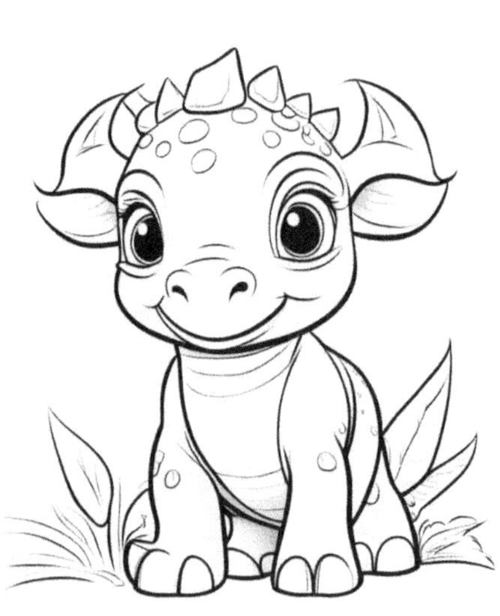

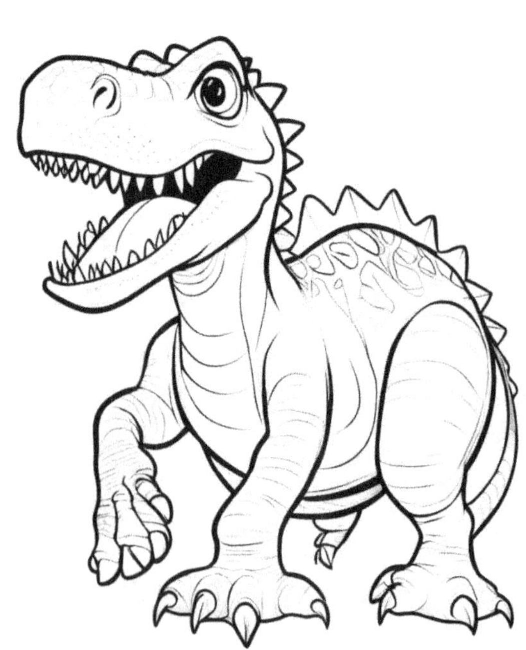

TEST YOUR COLOR

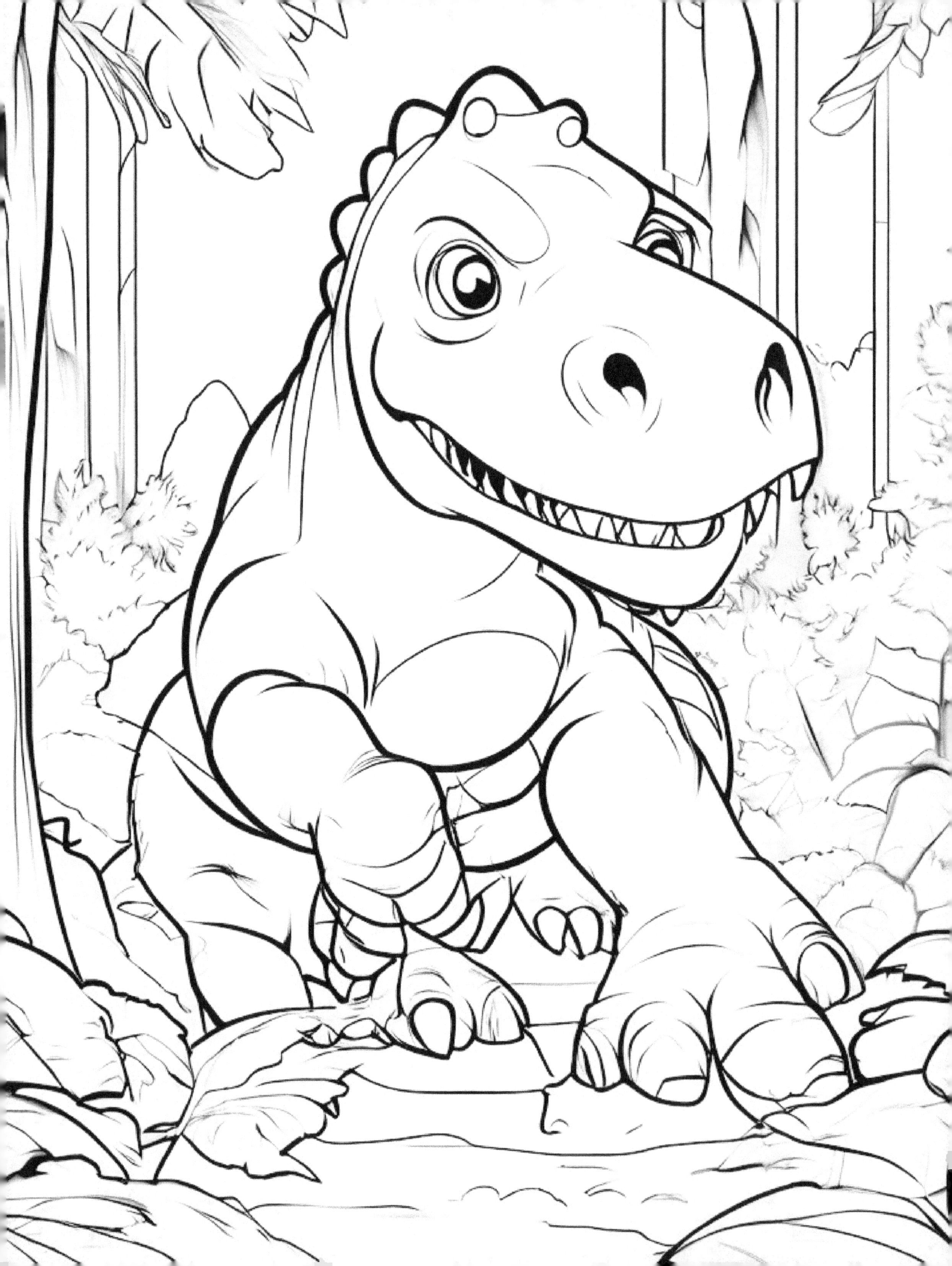

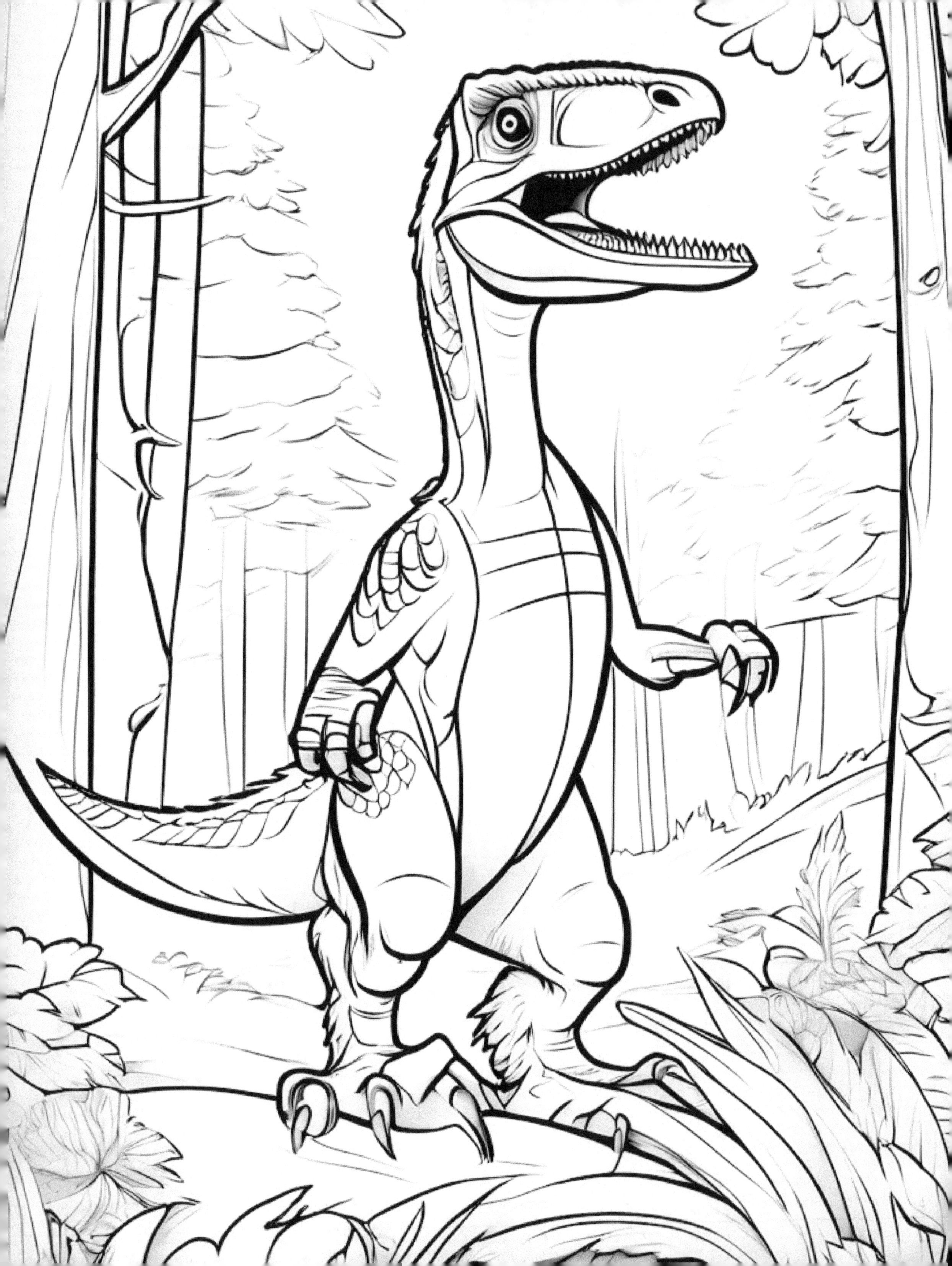

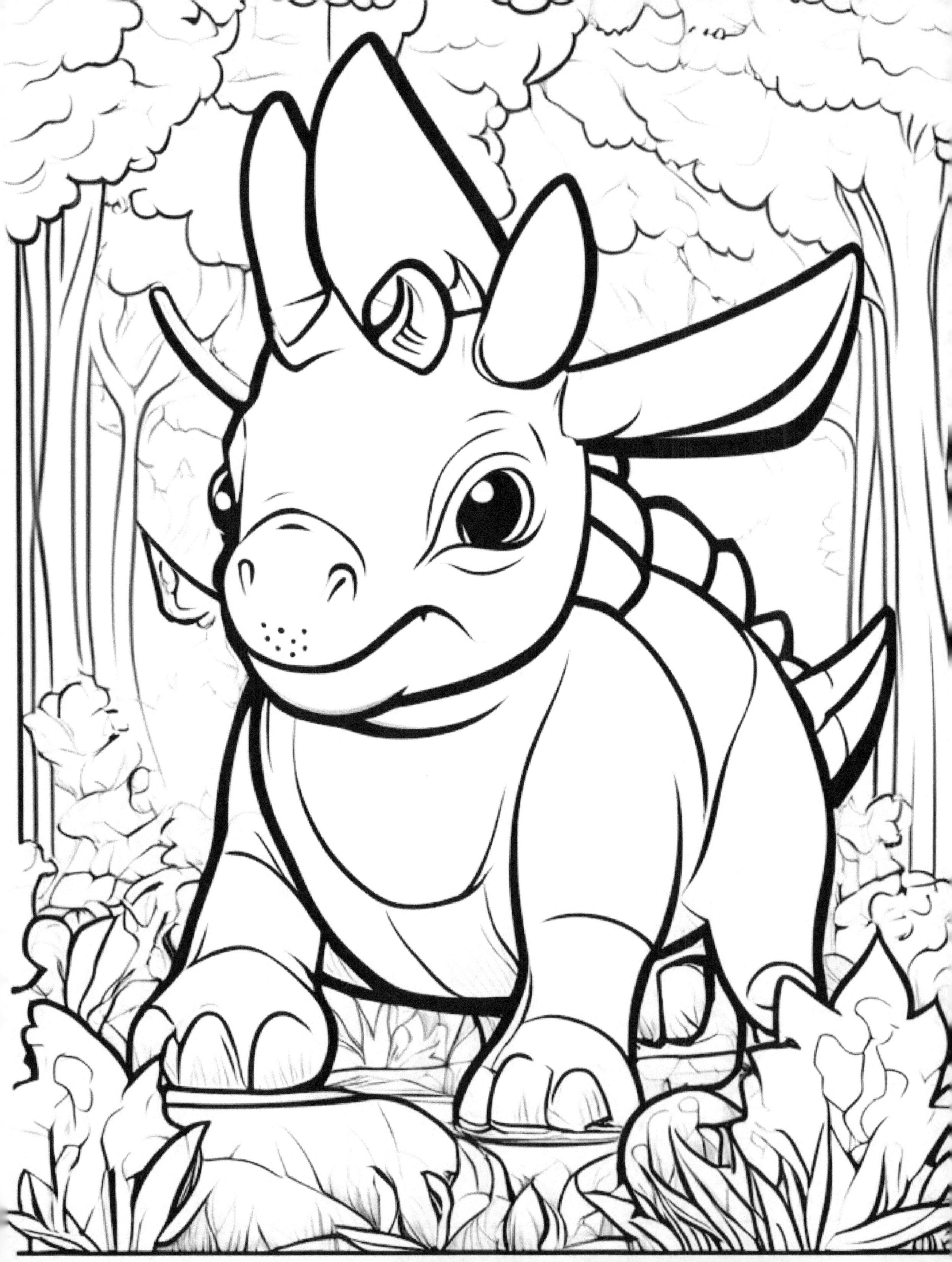

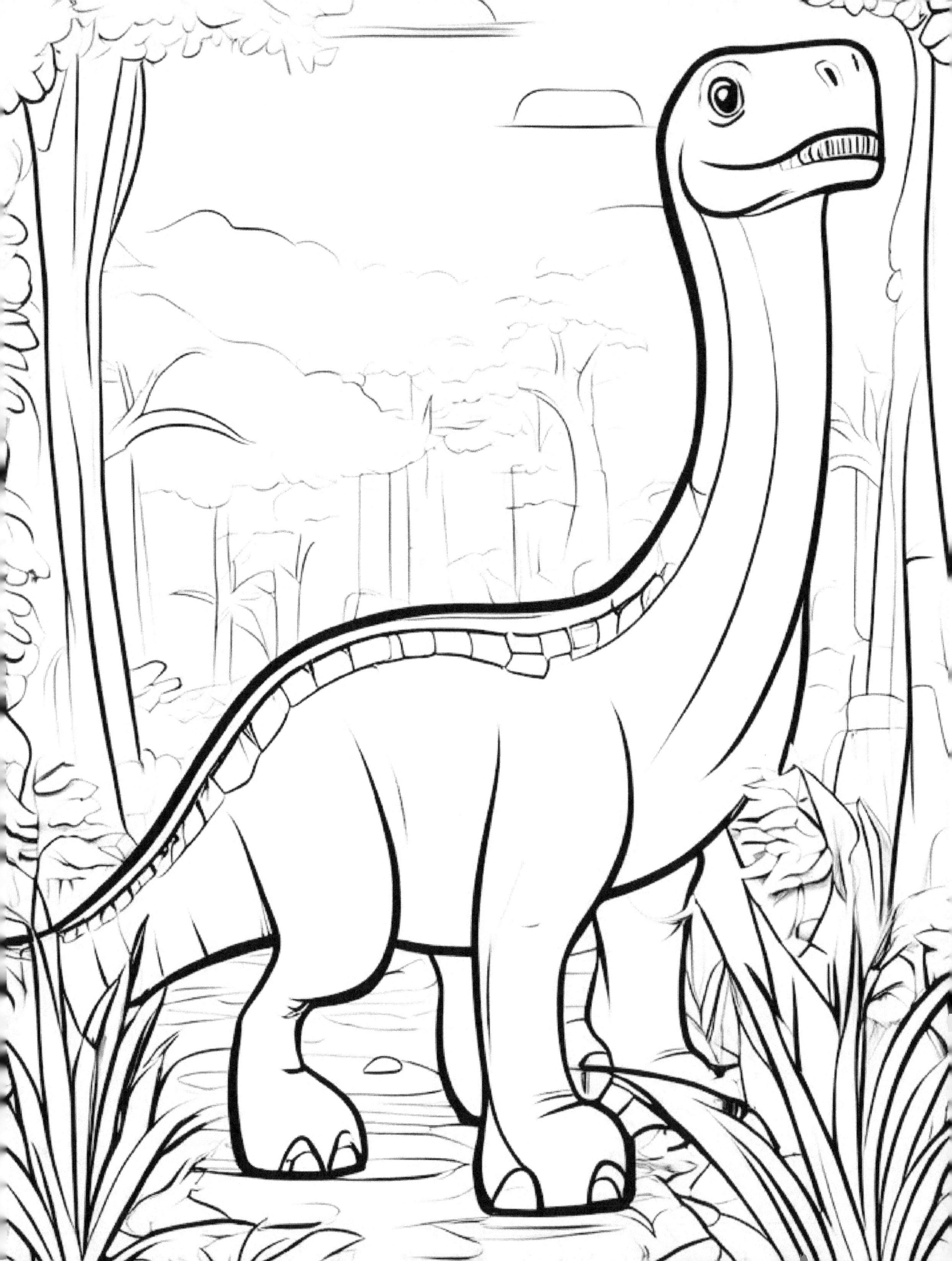

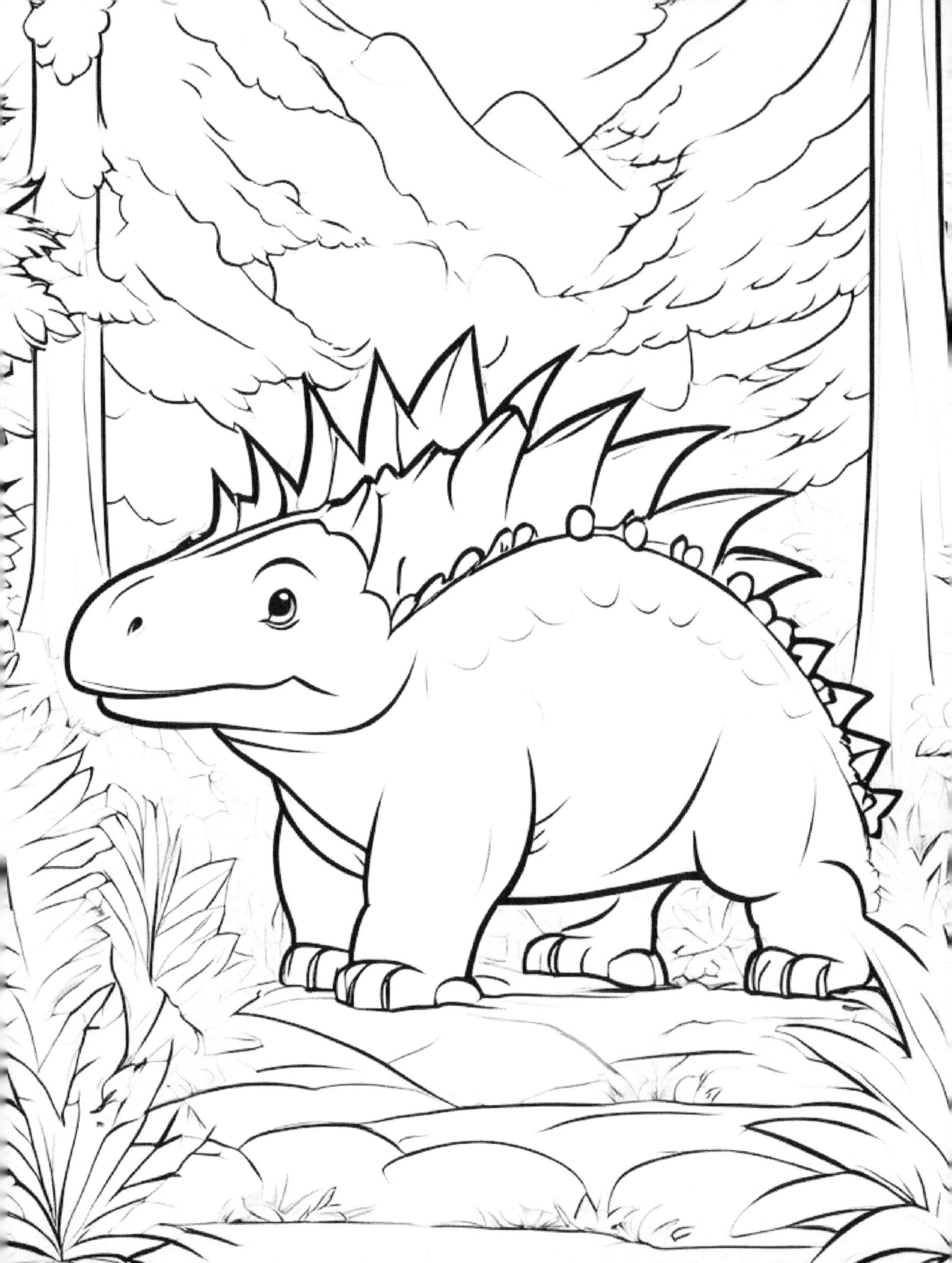

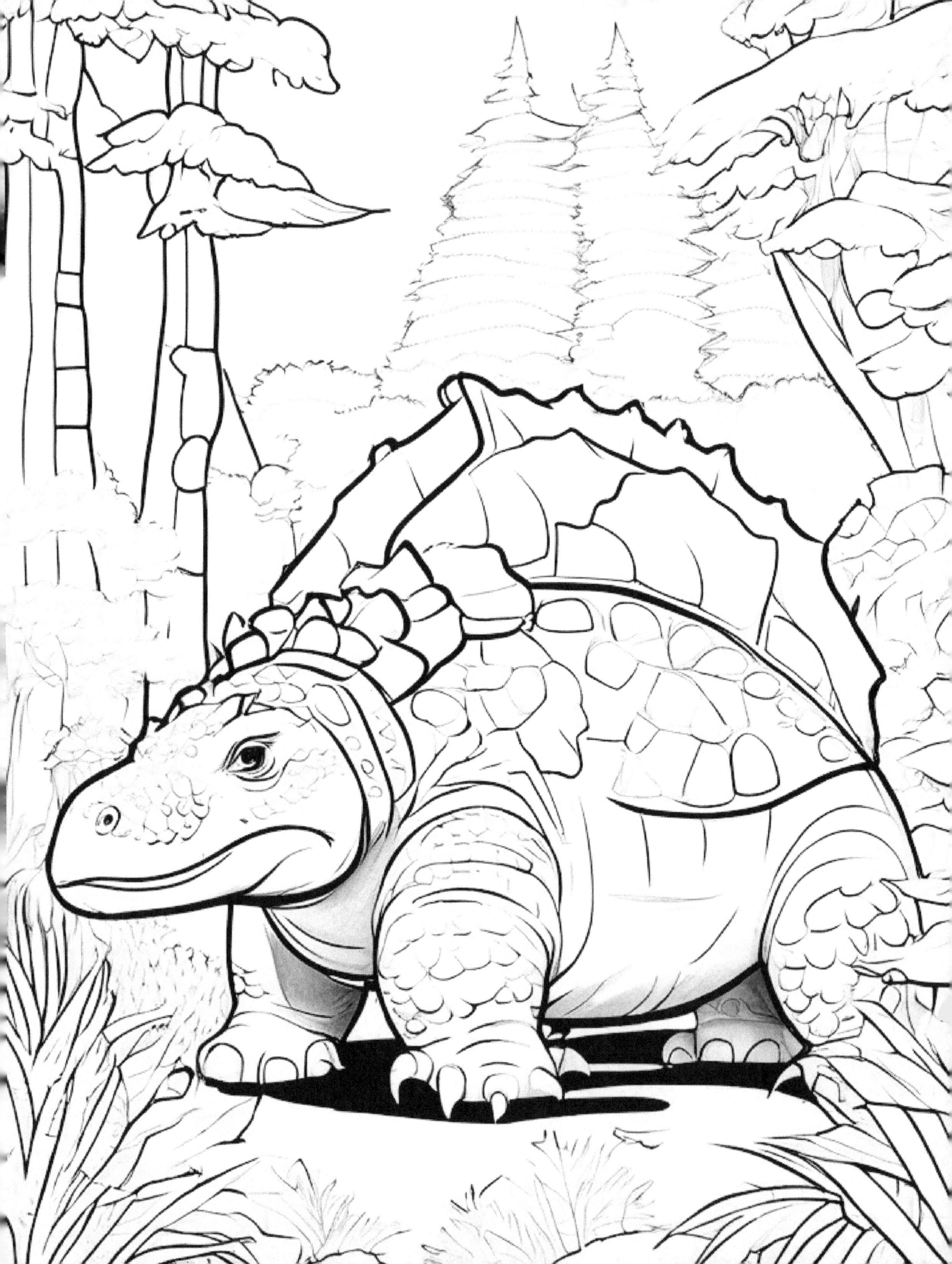

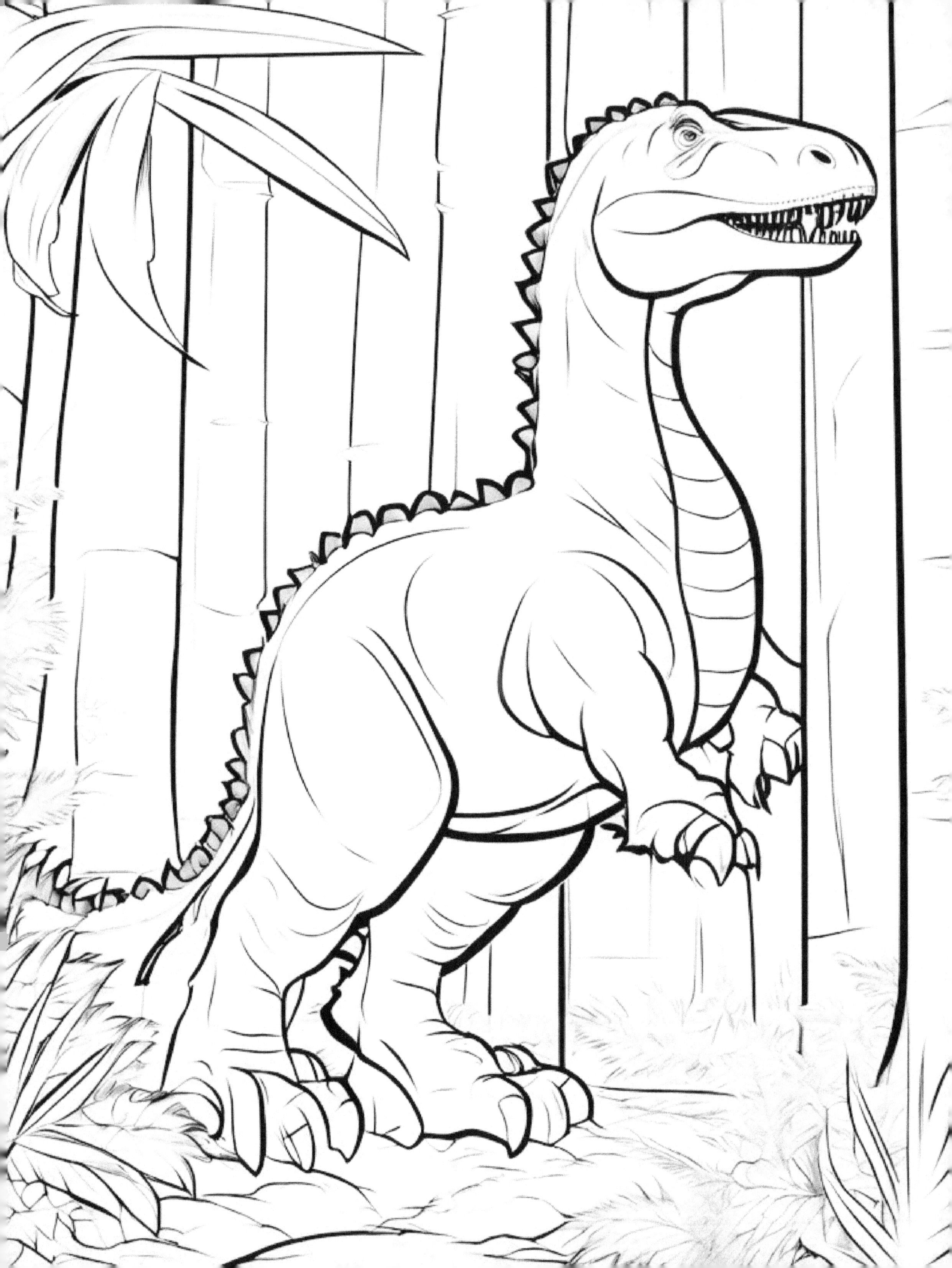

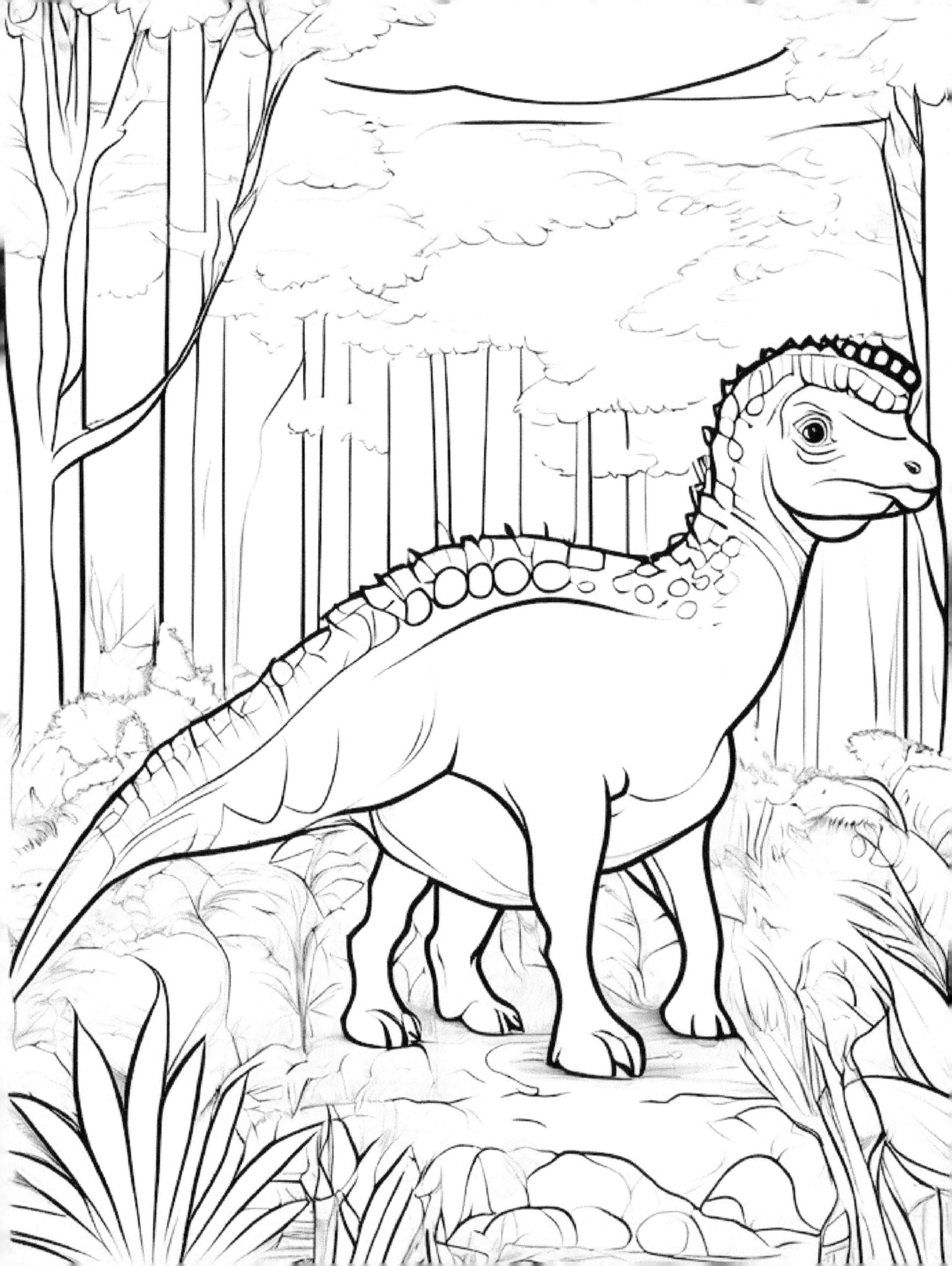

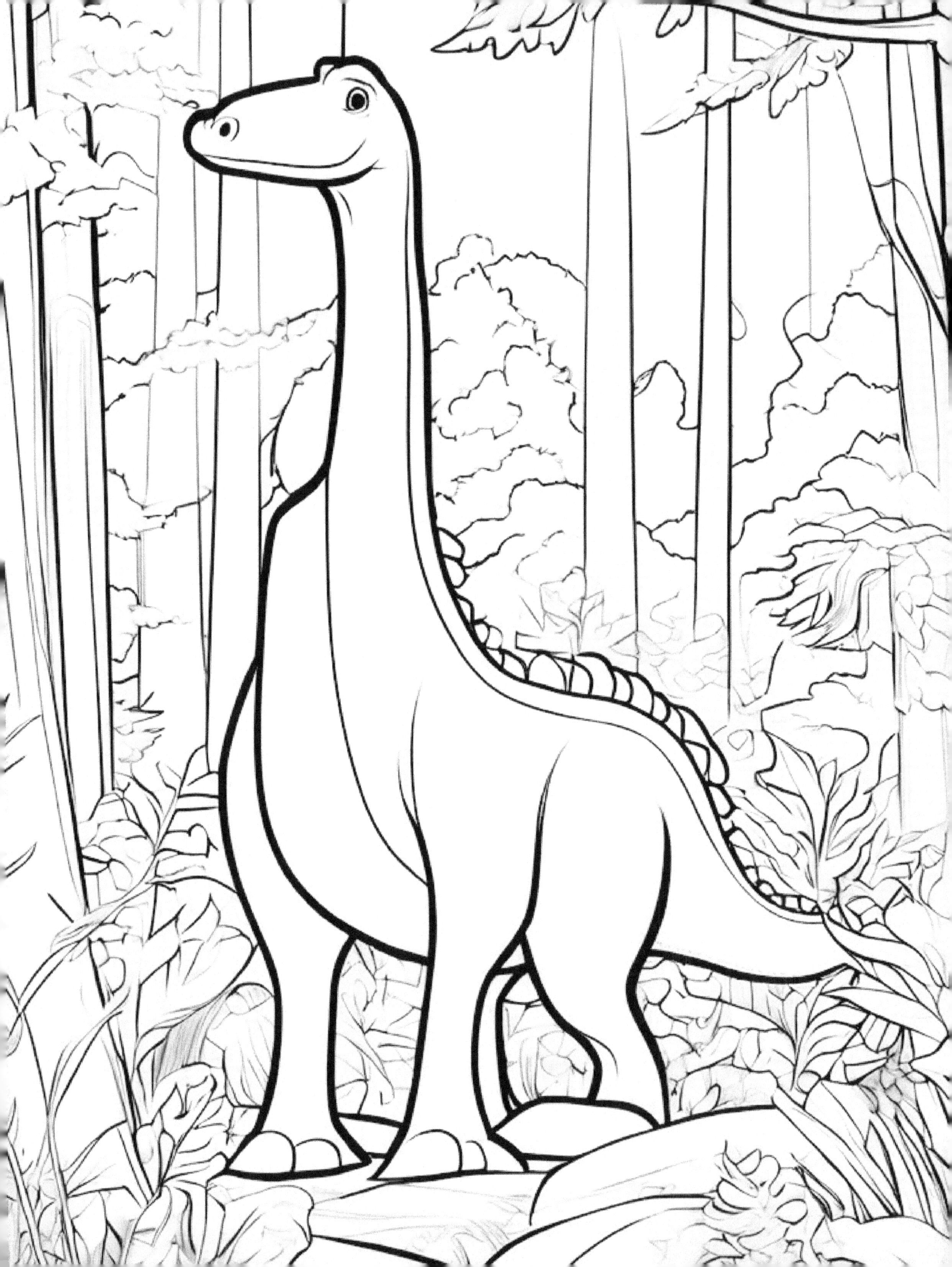

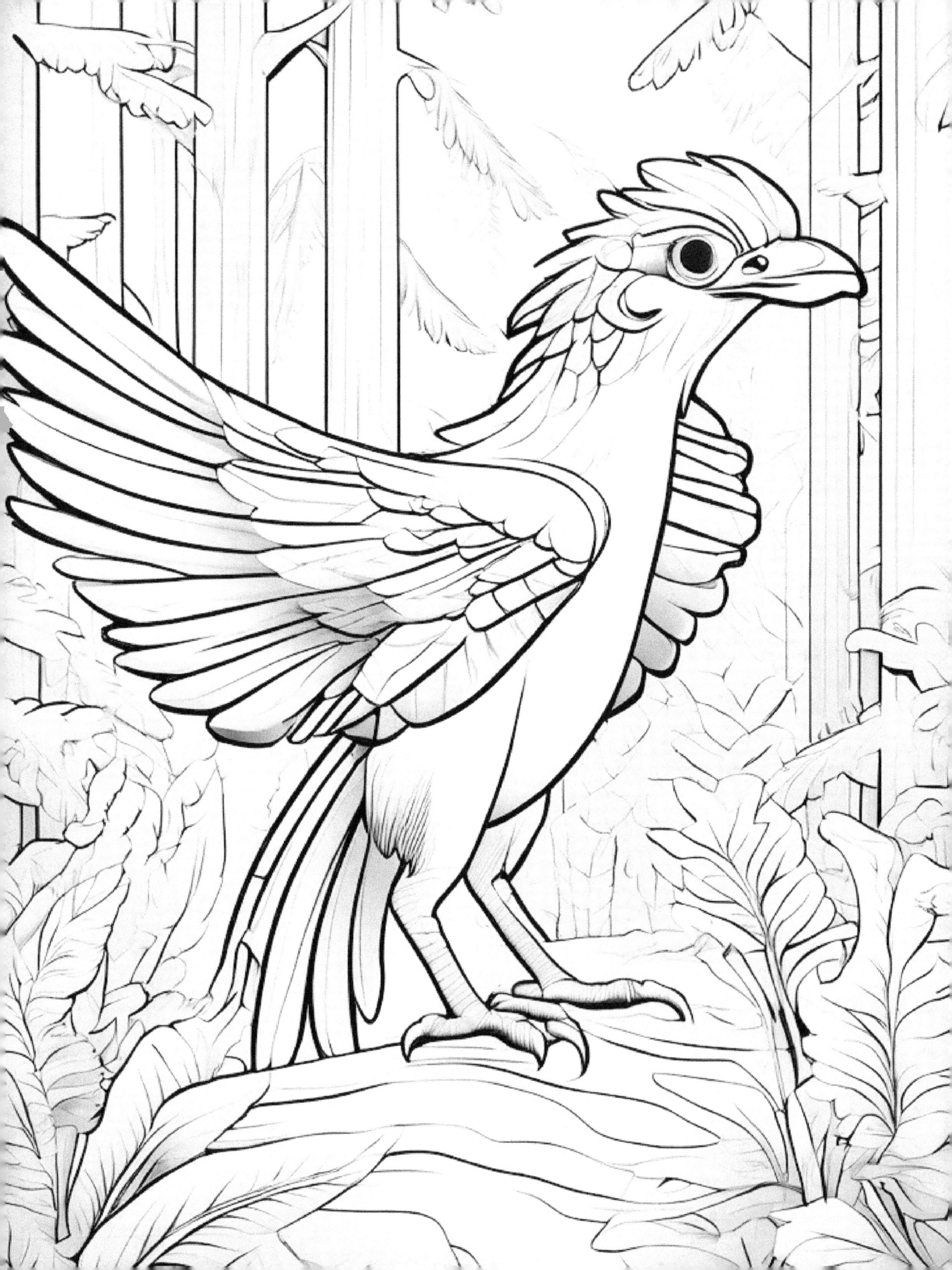

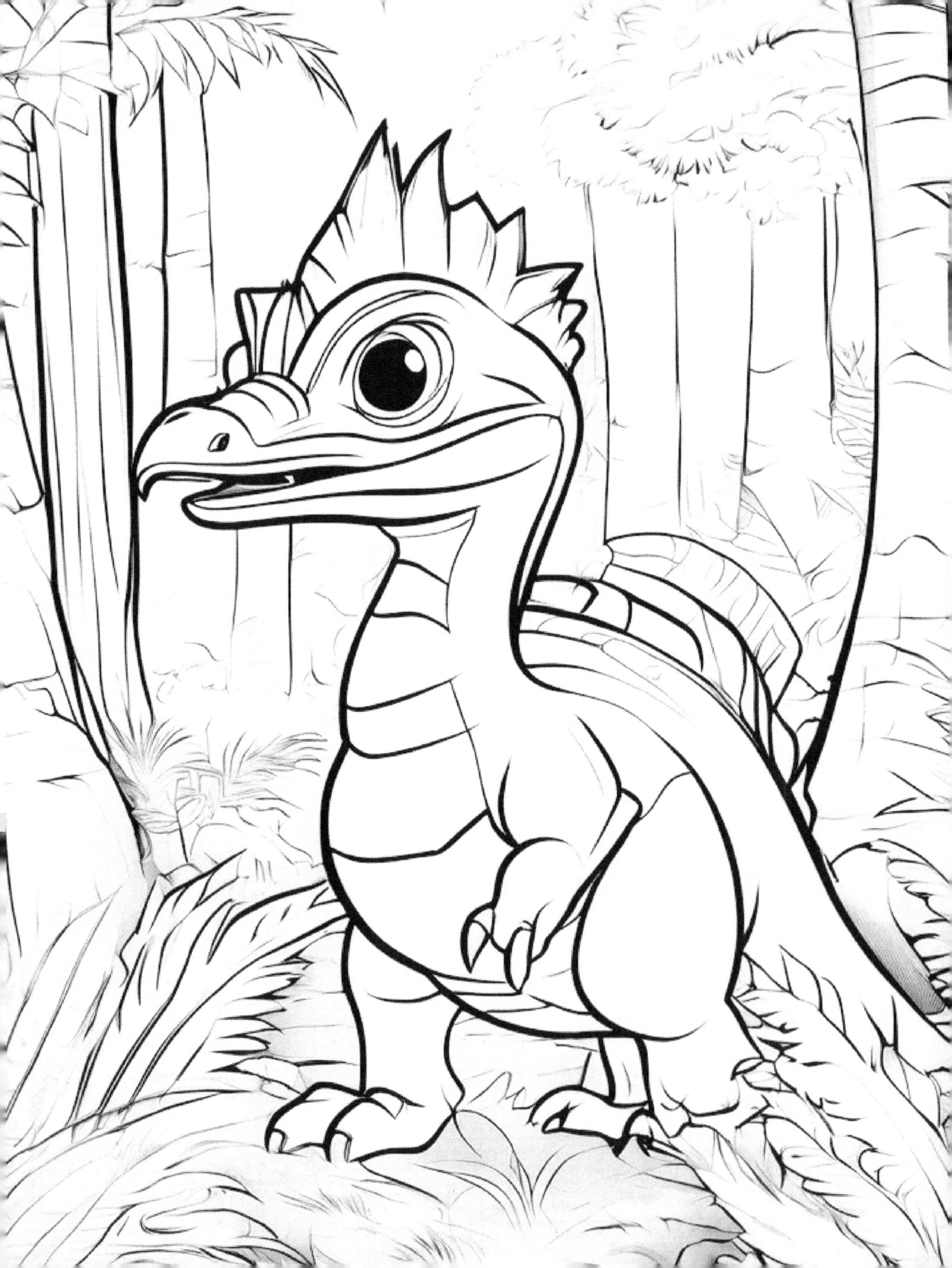

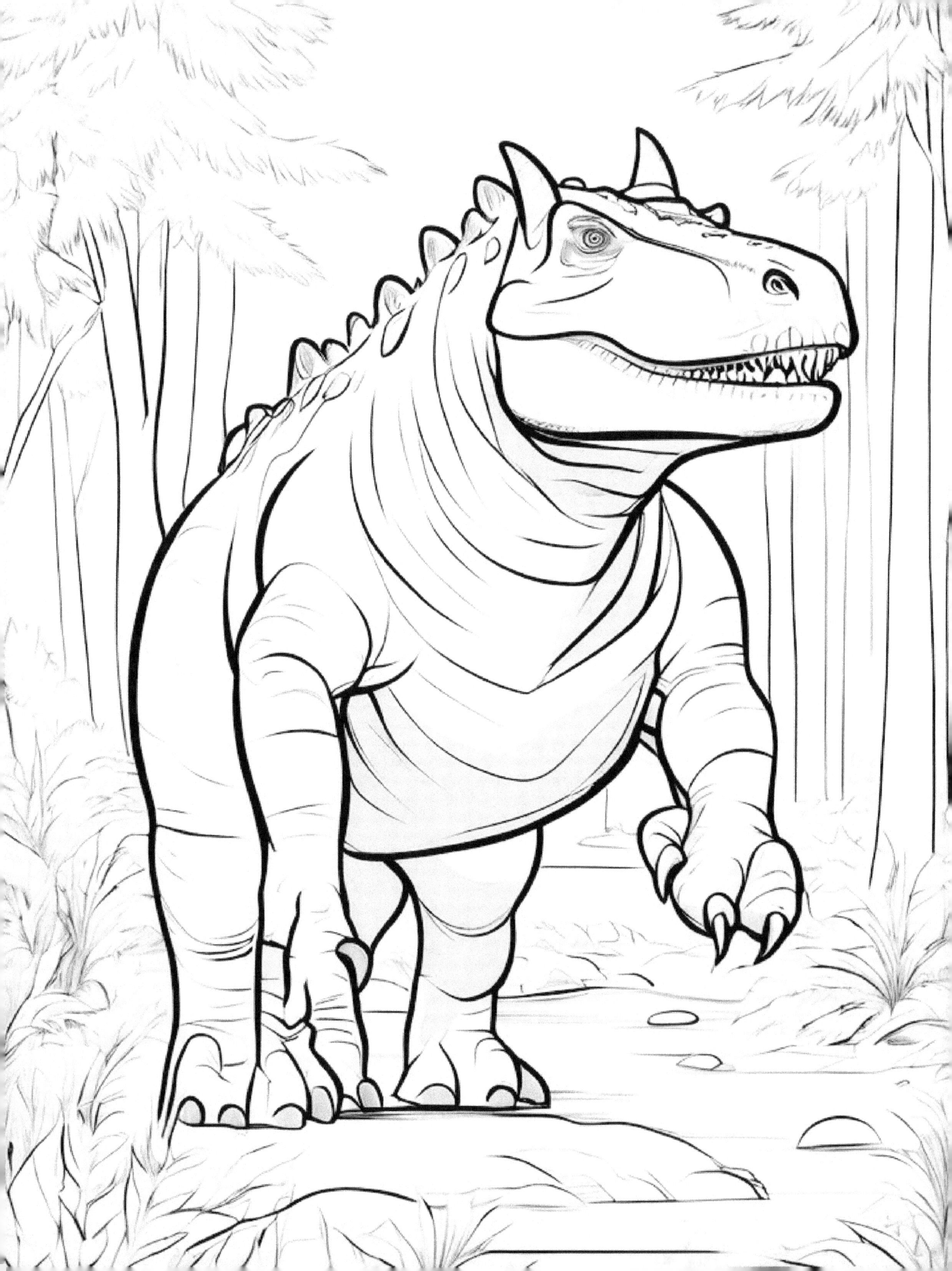

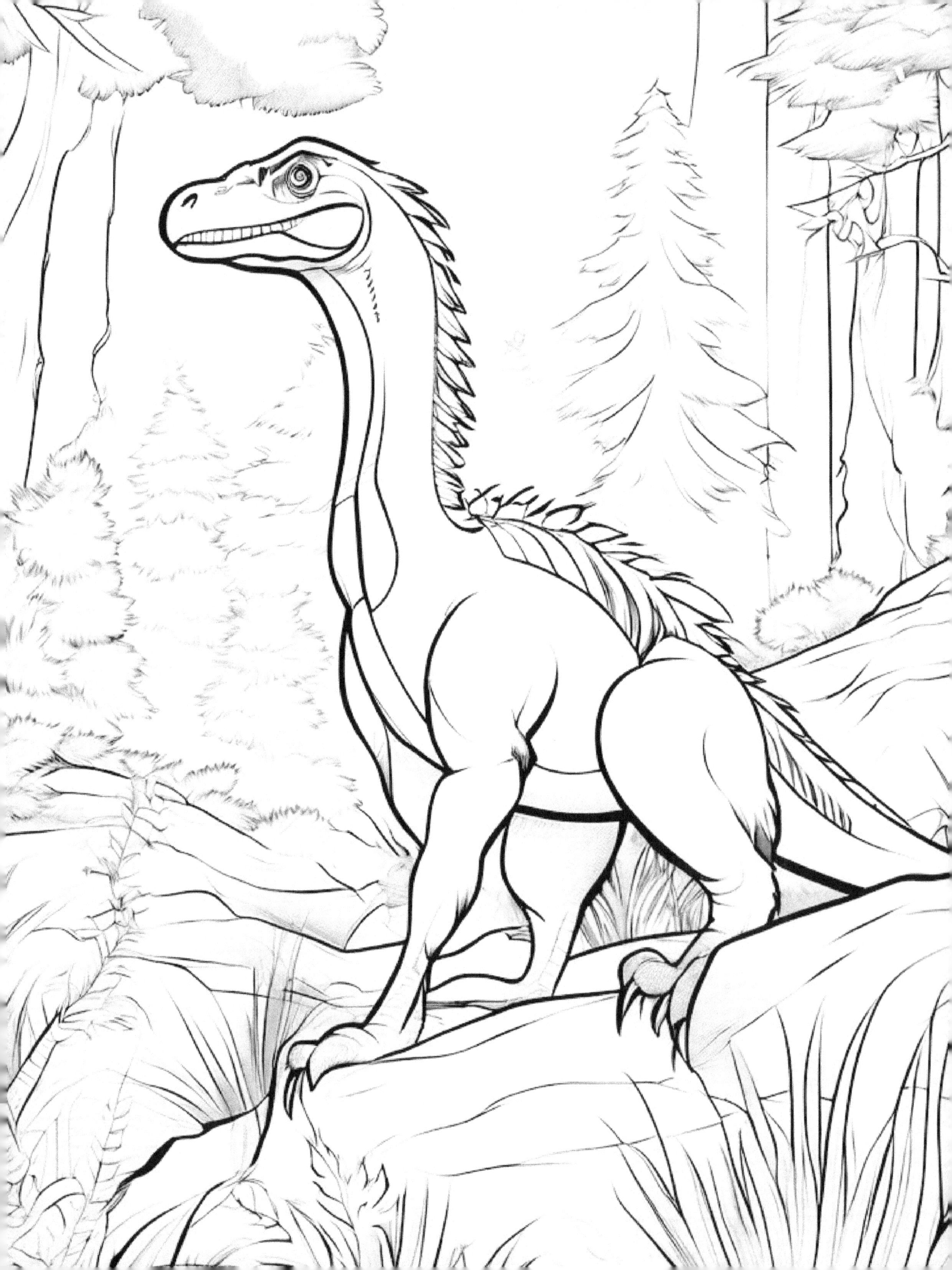

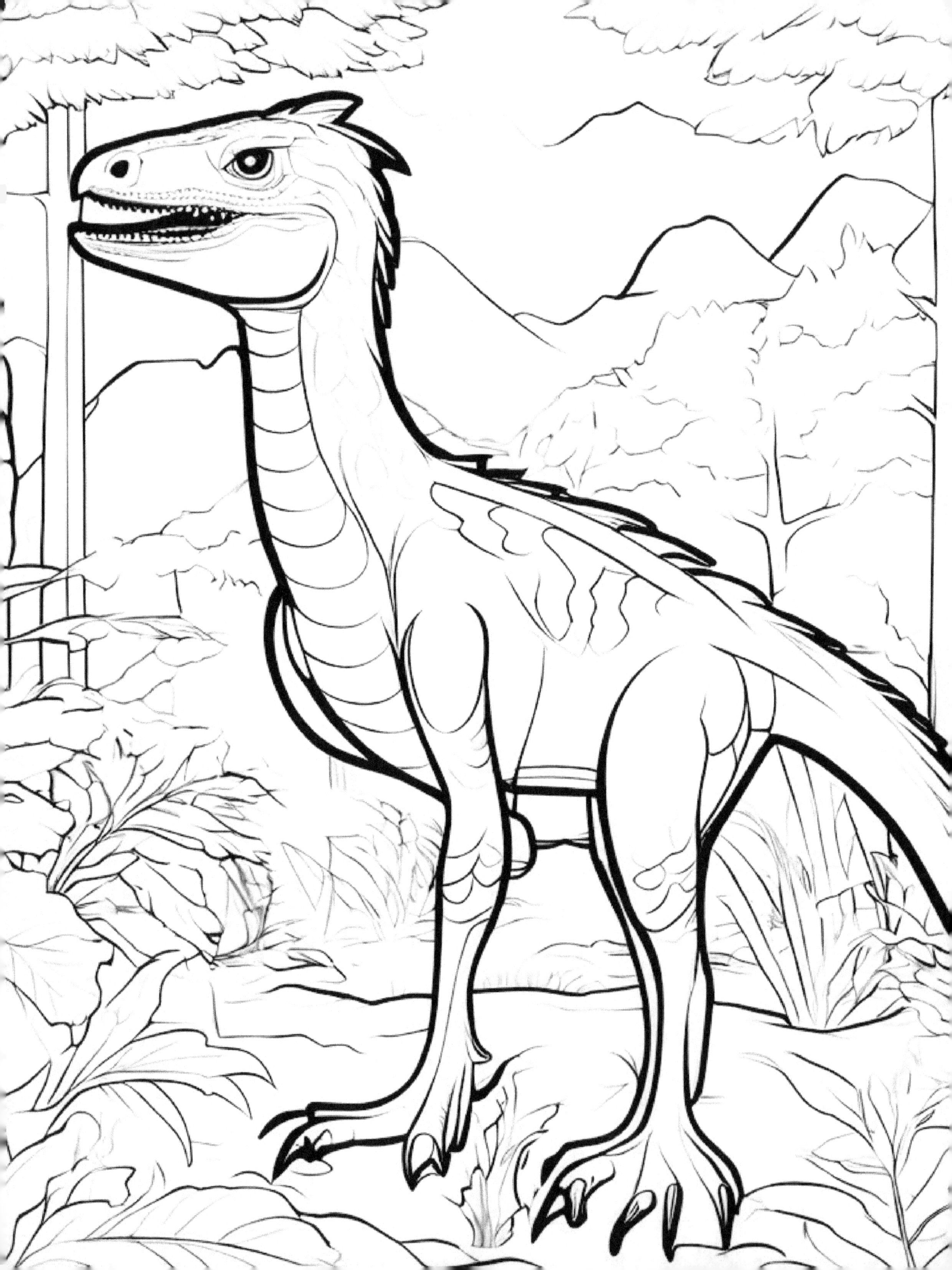

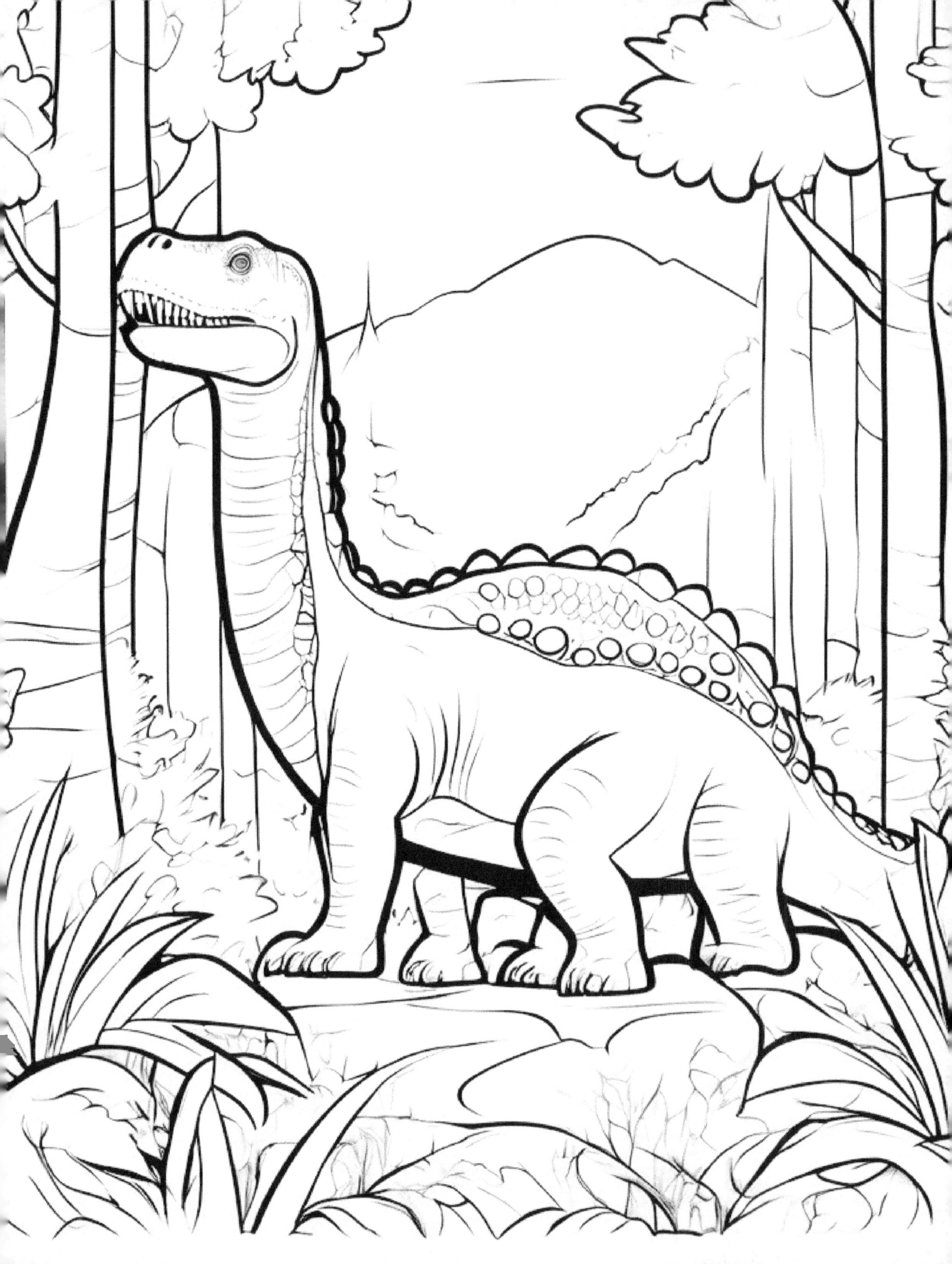

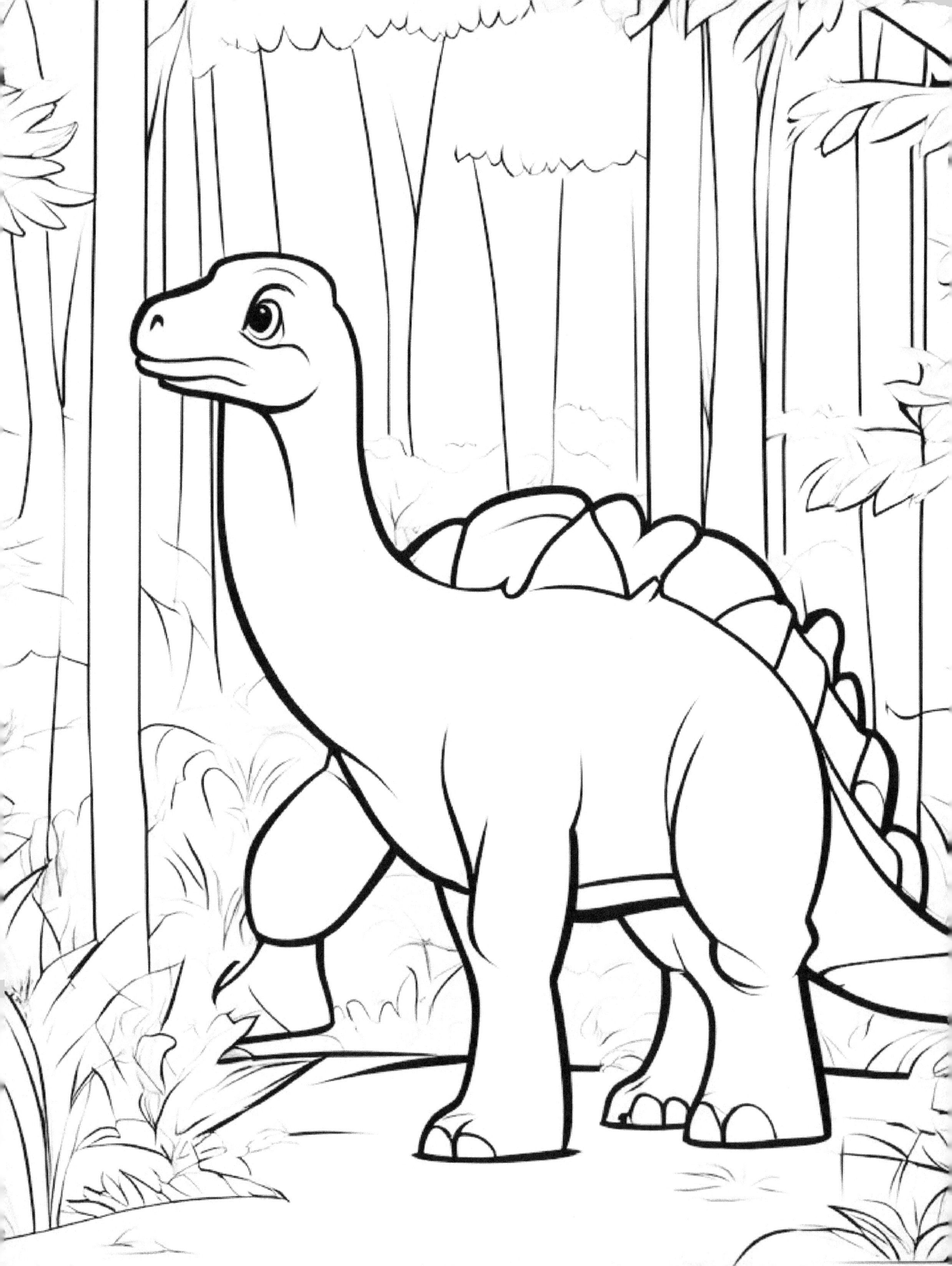

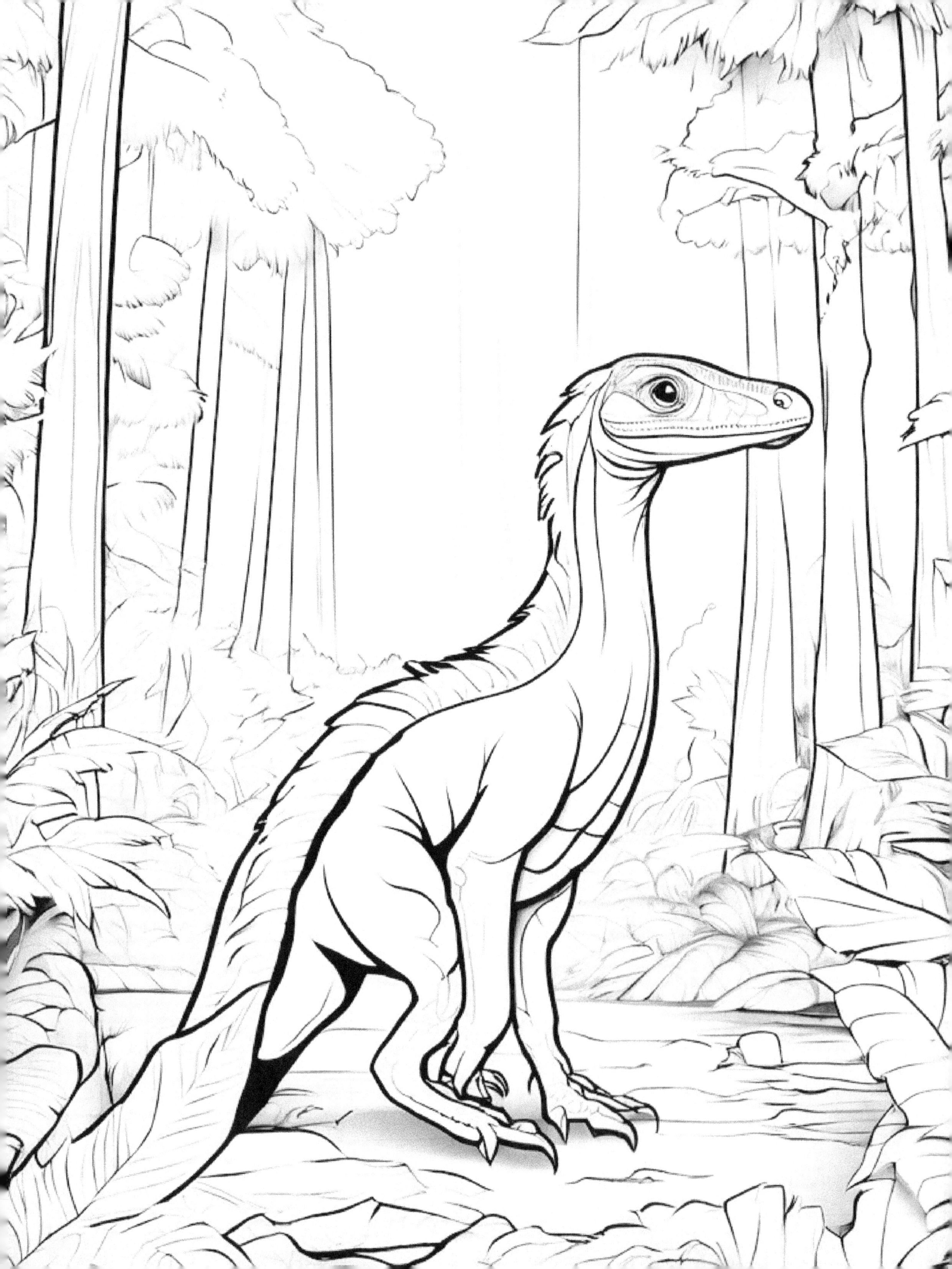

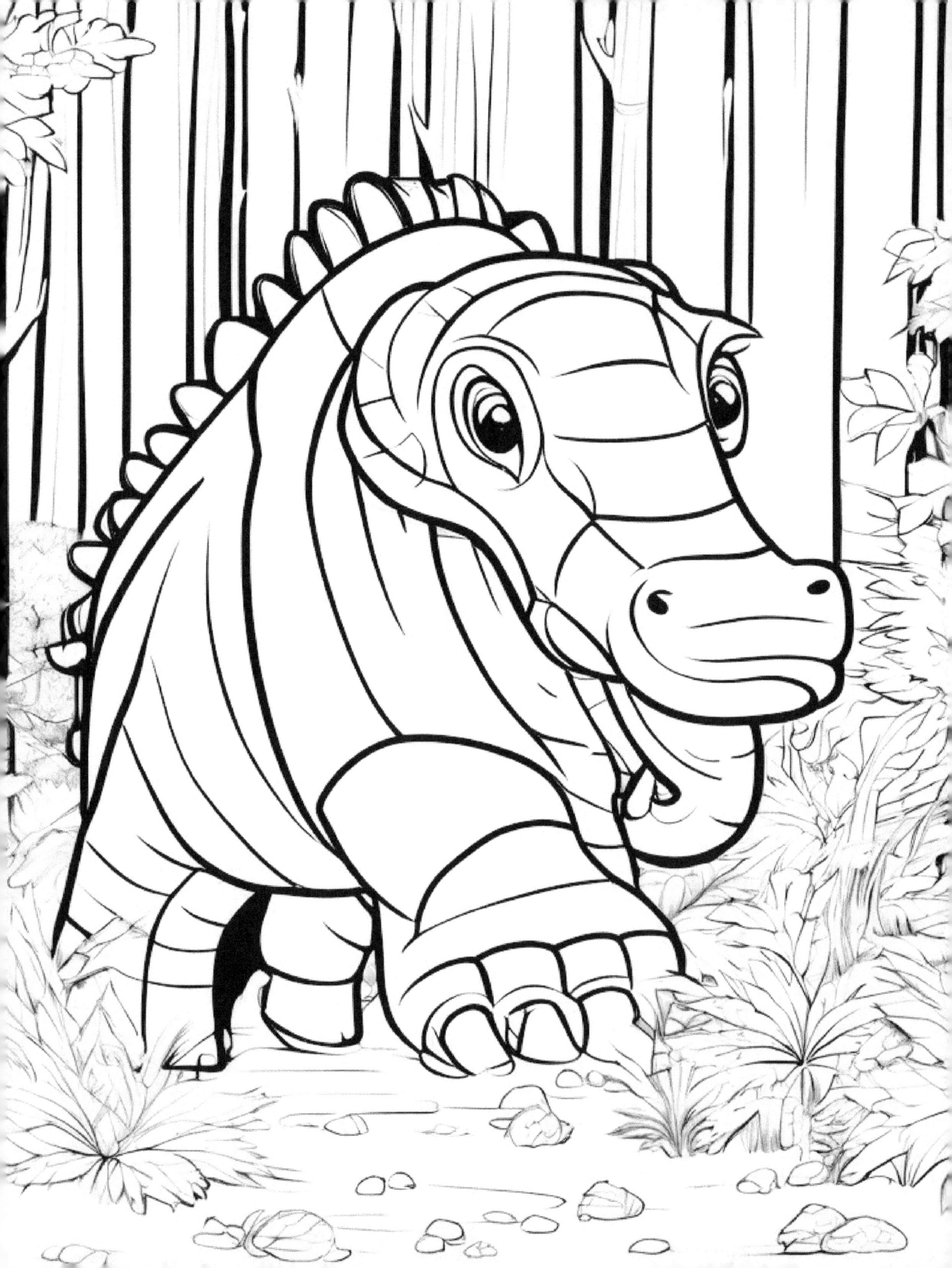

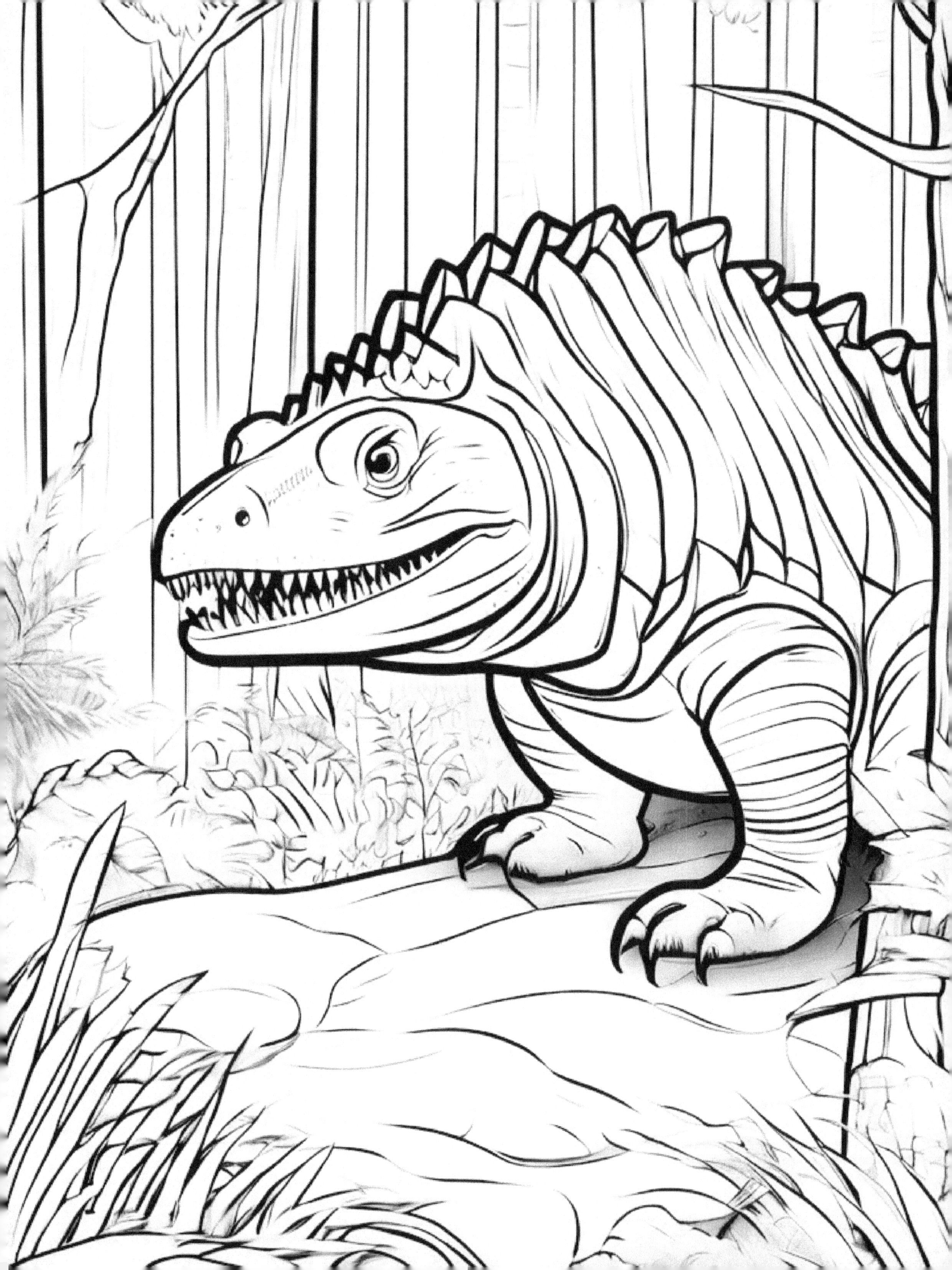

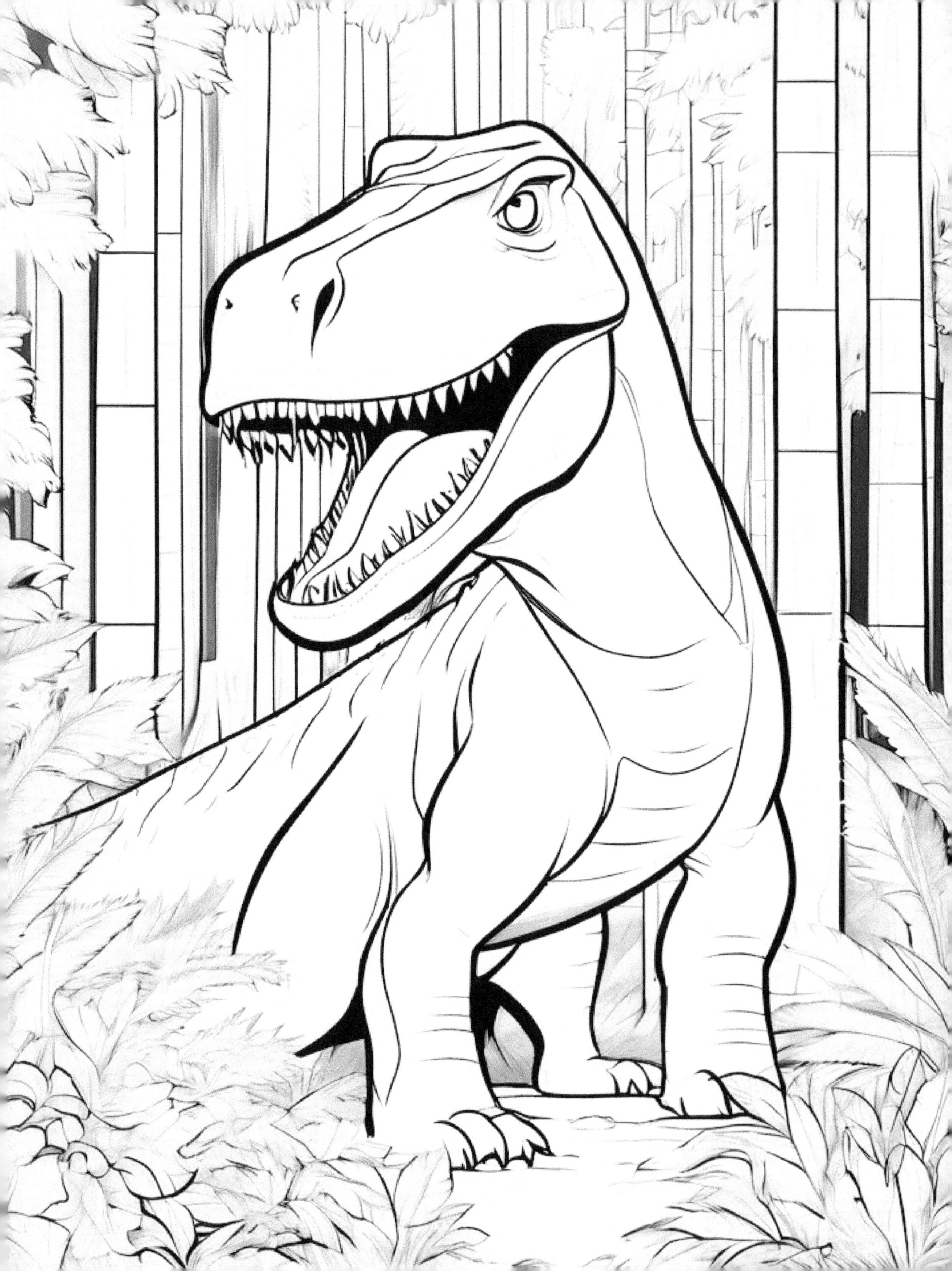

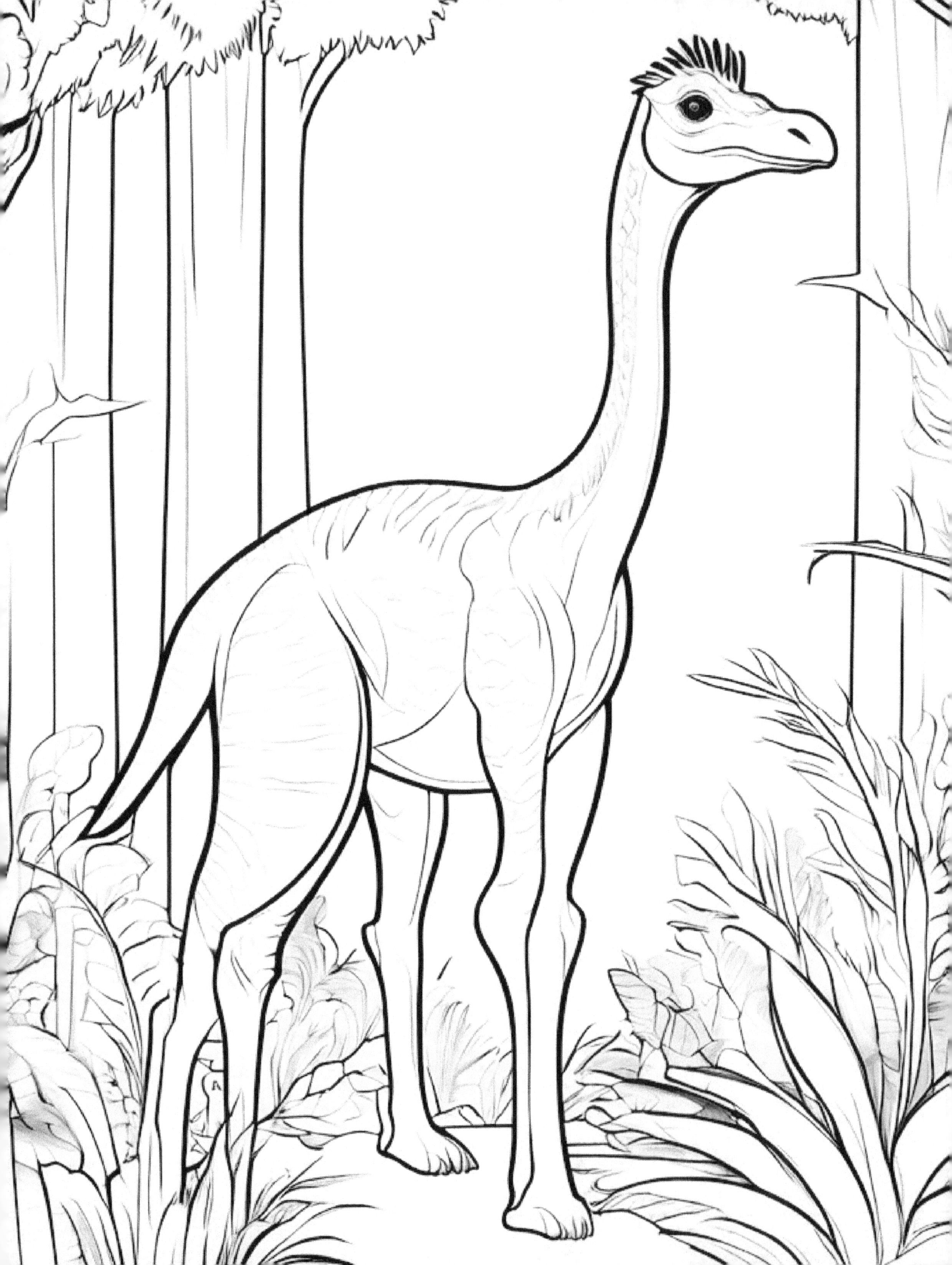

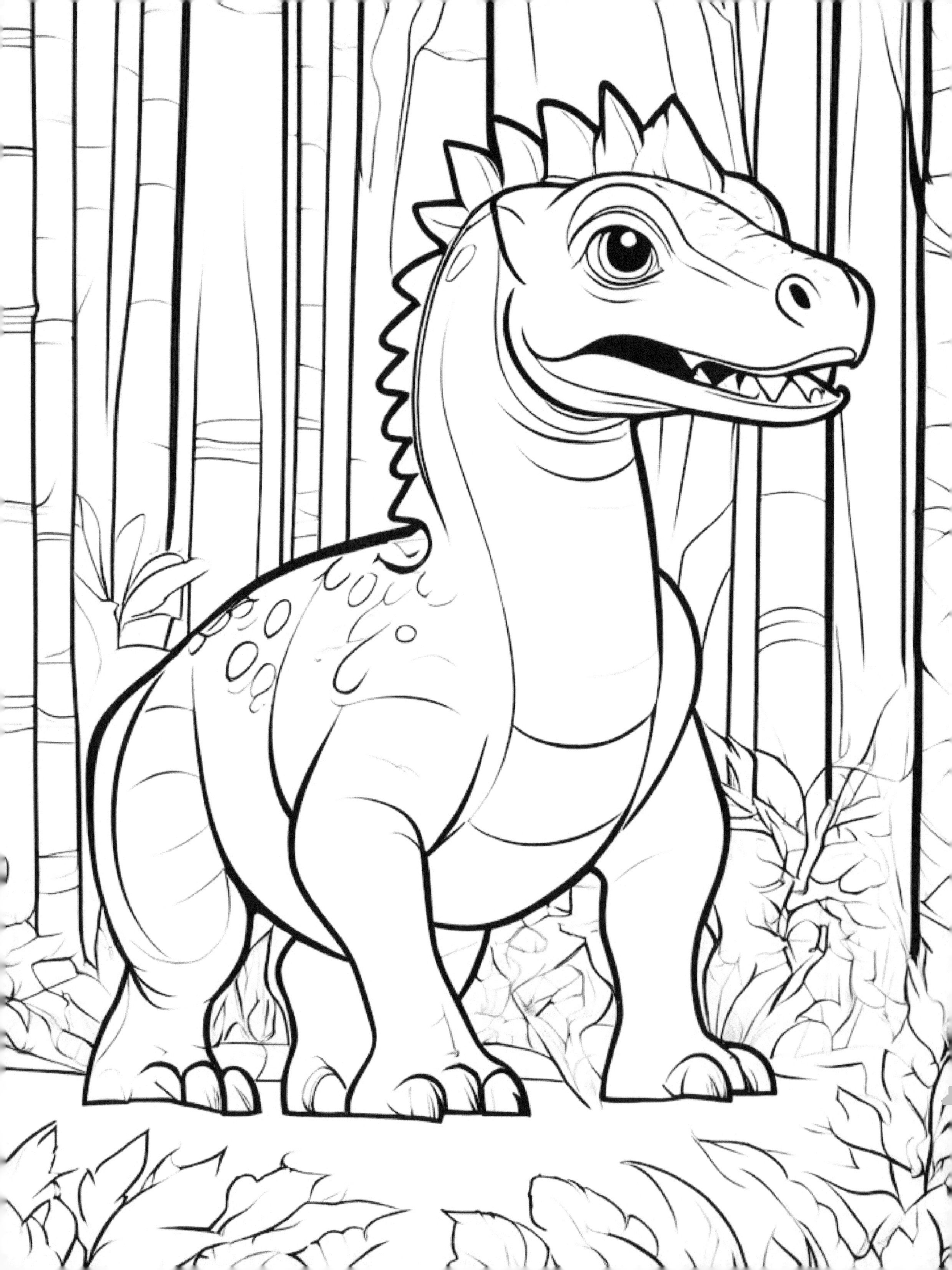

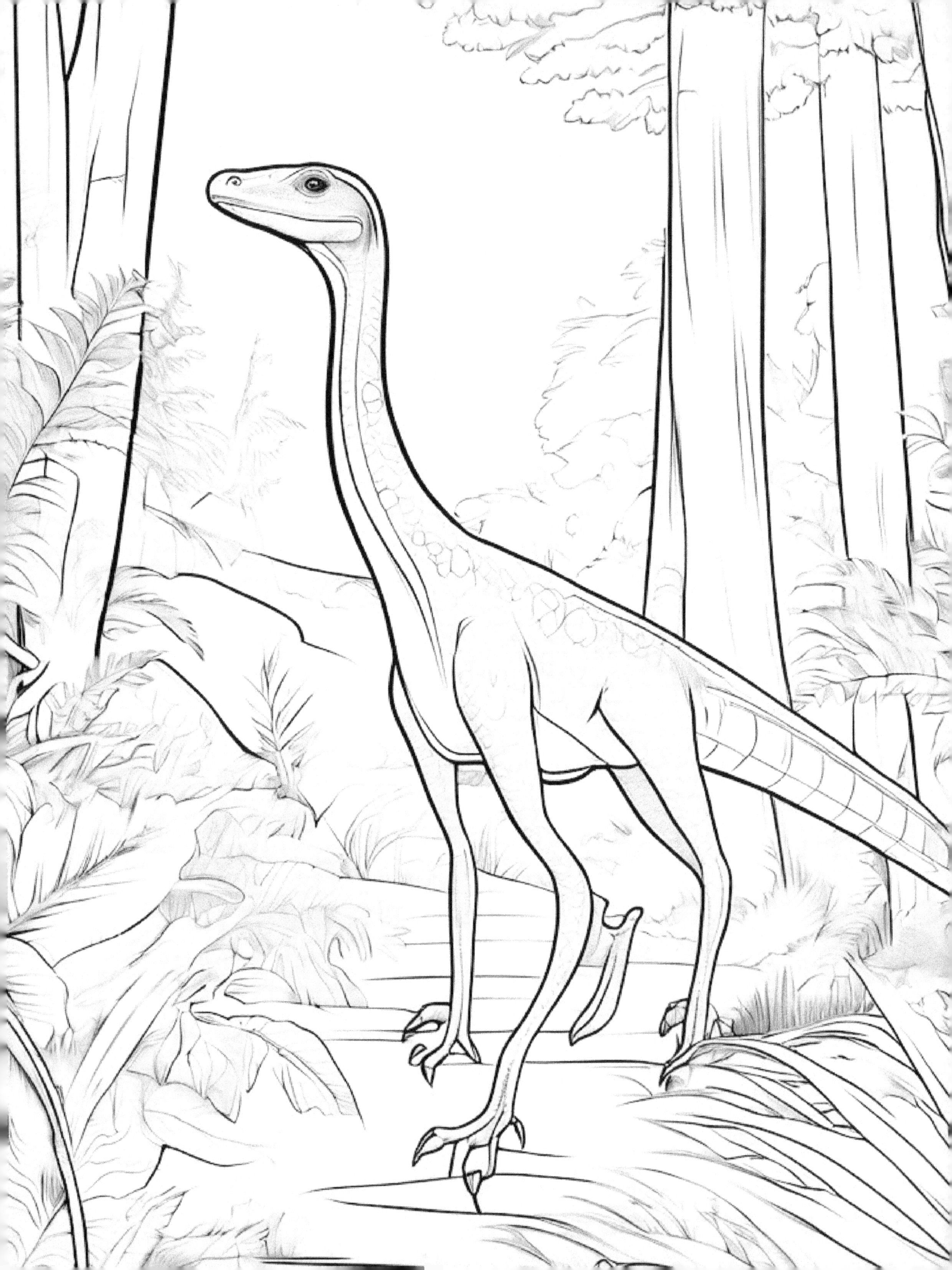

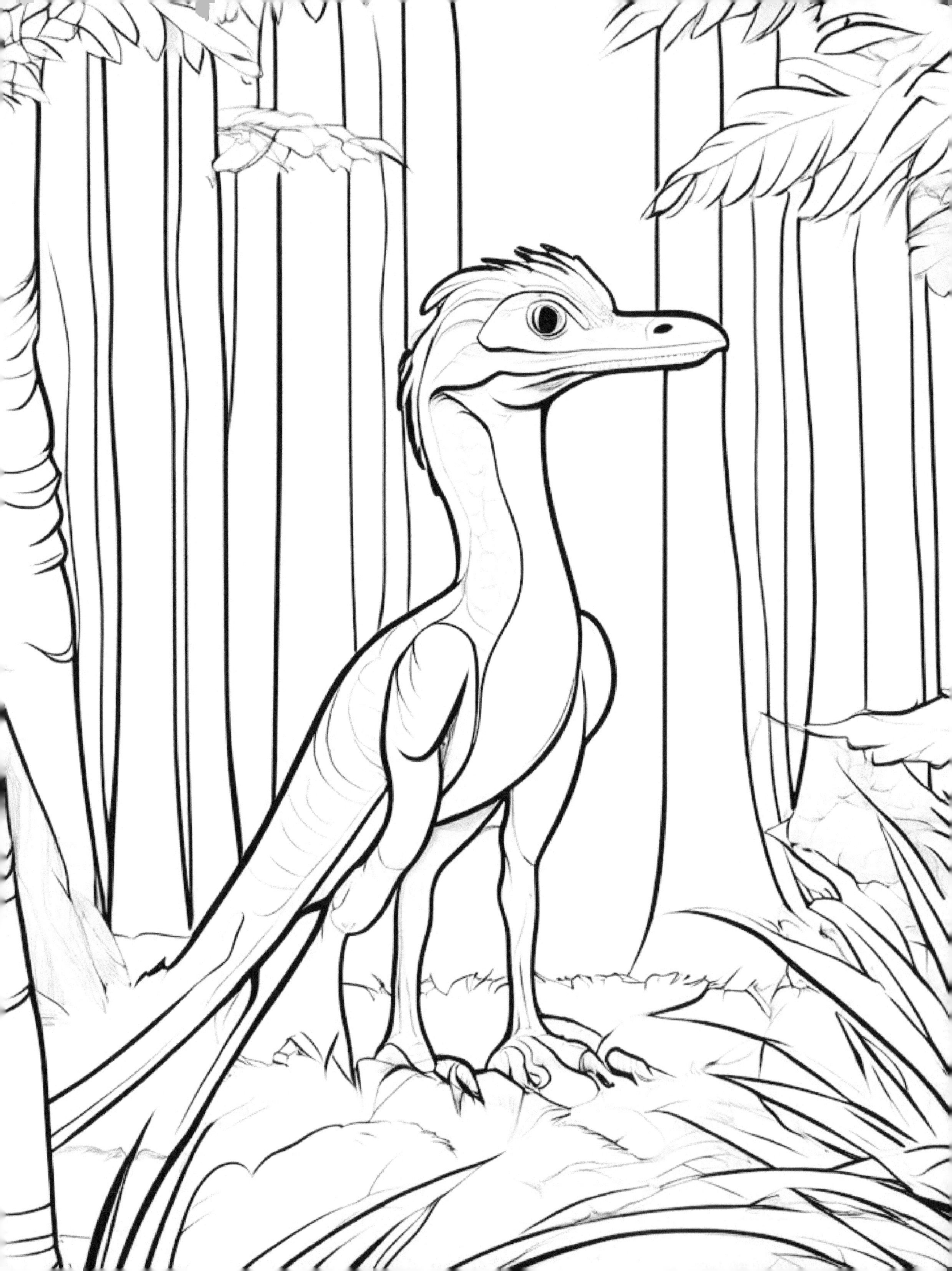

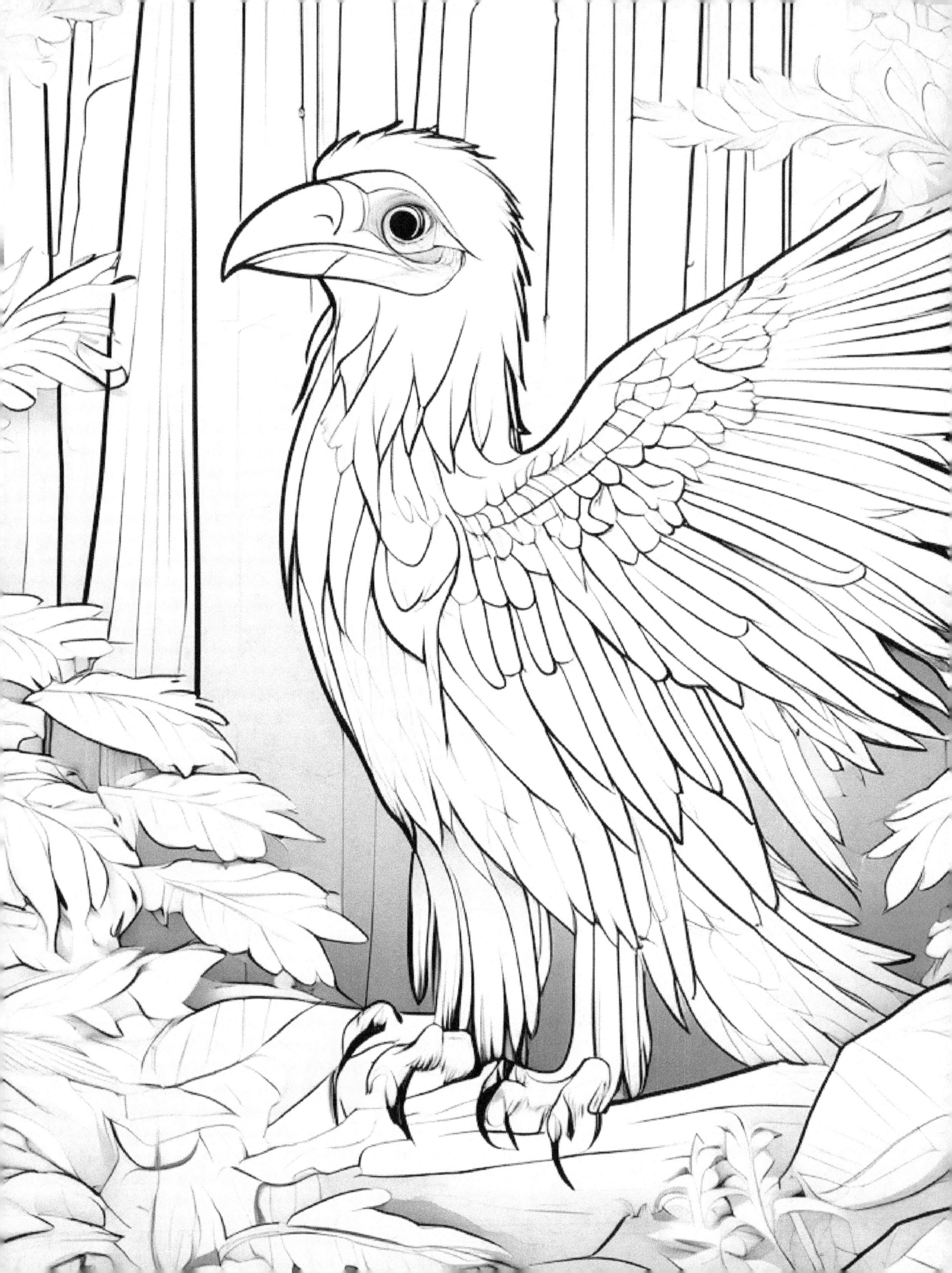

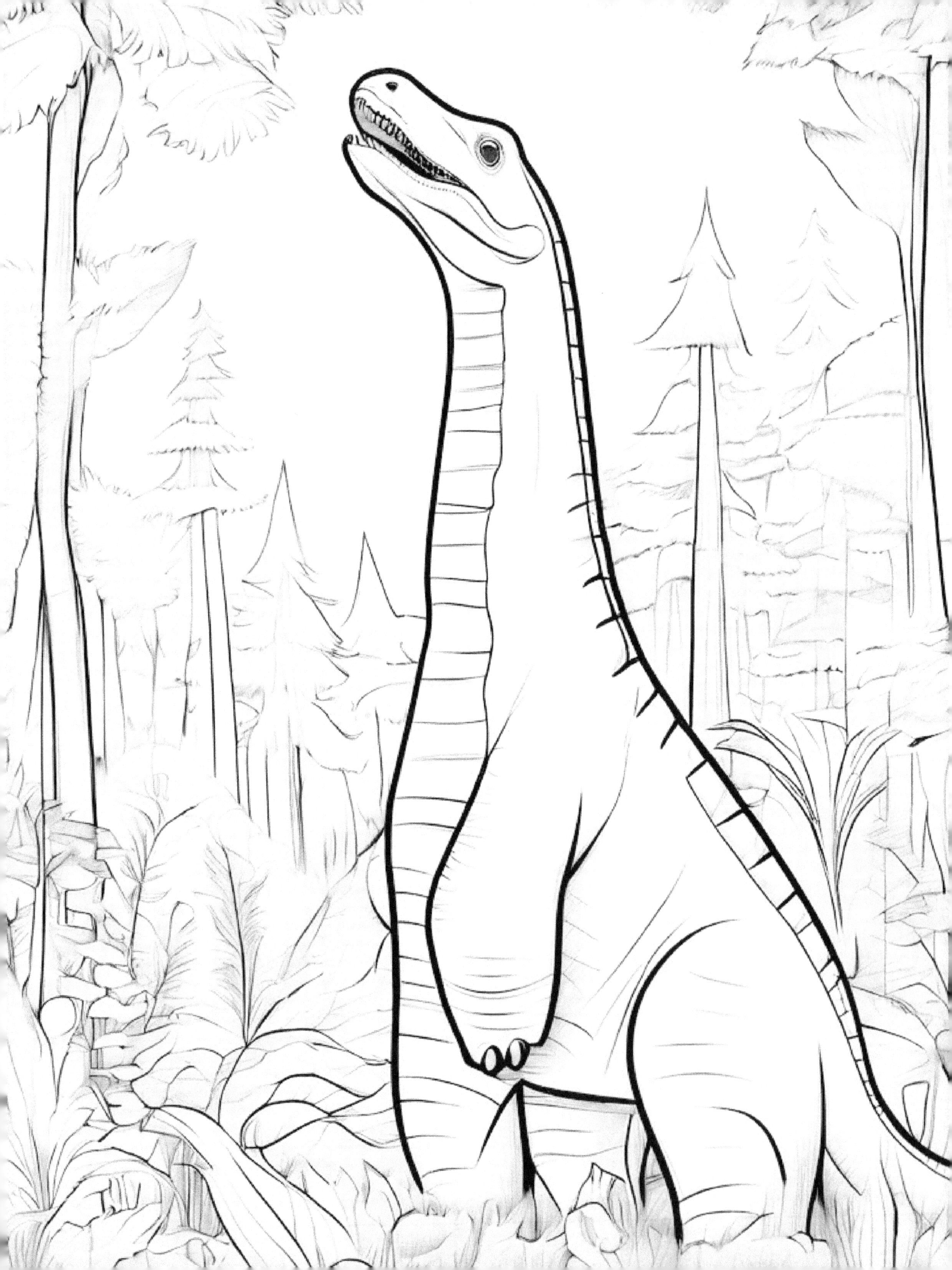

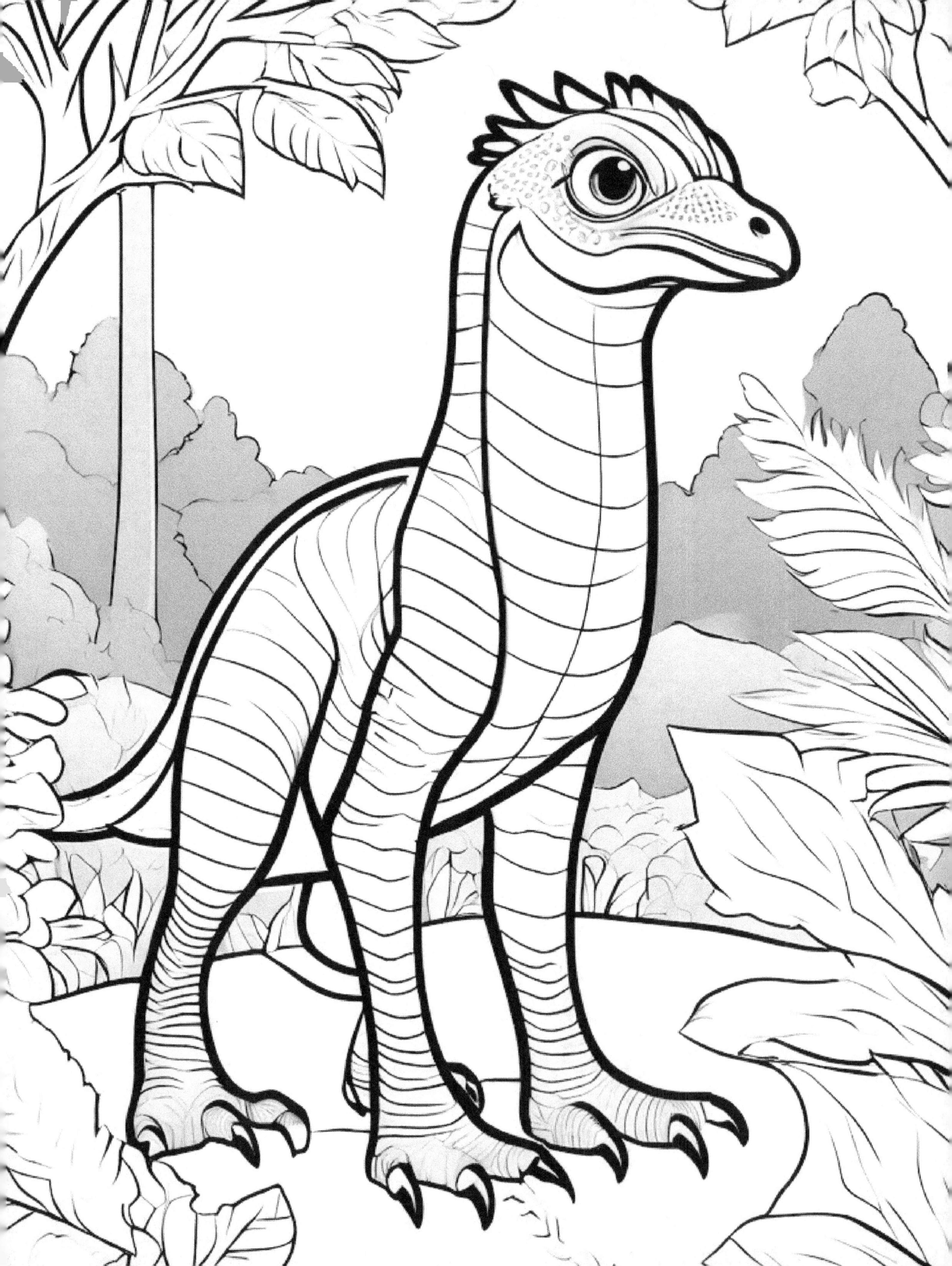

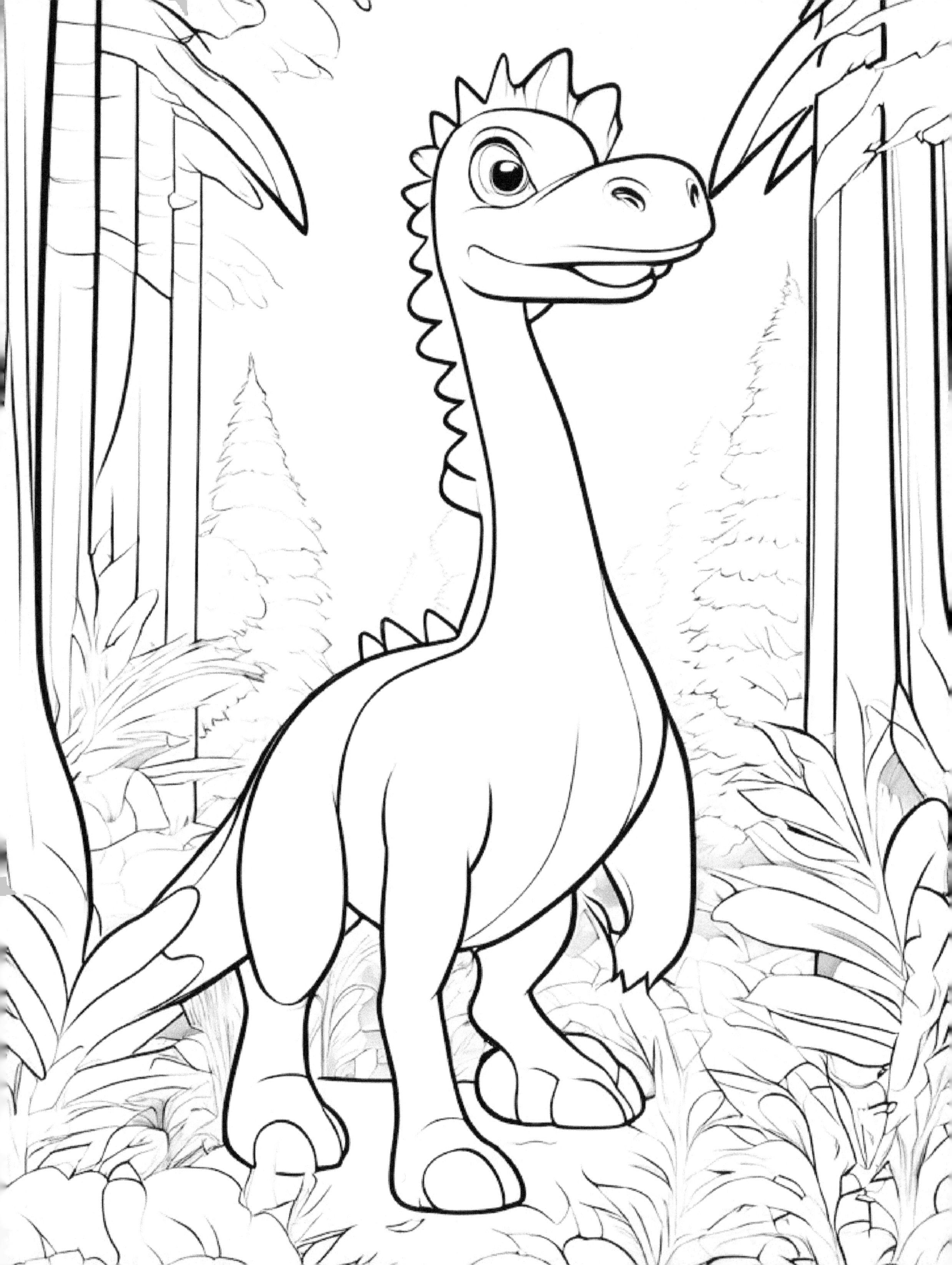

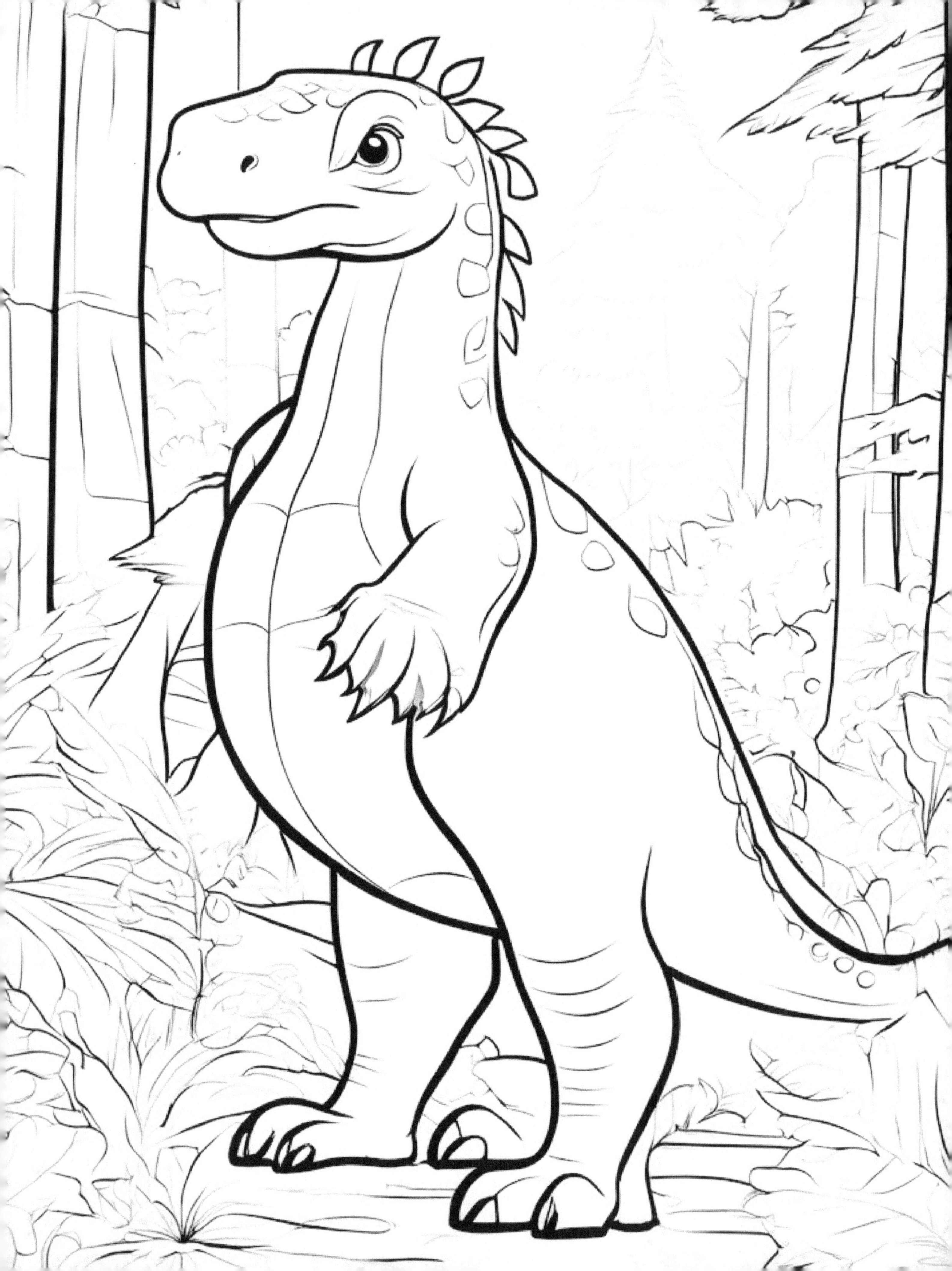

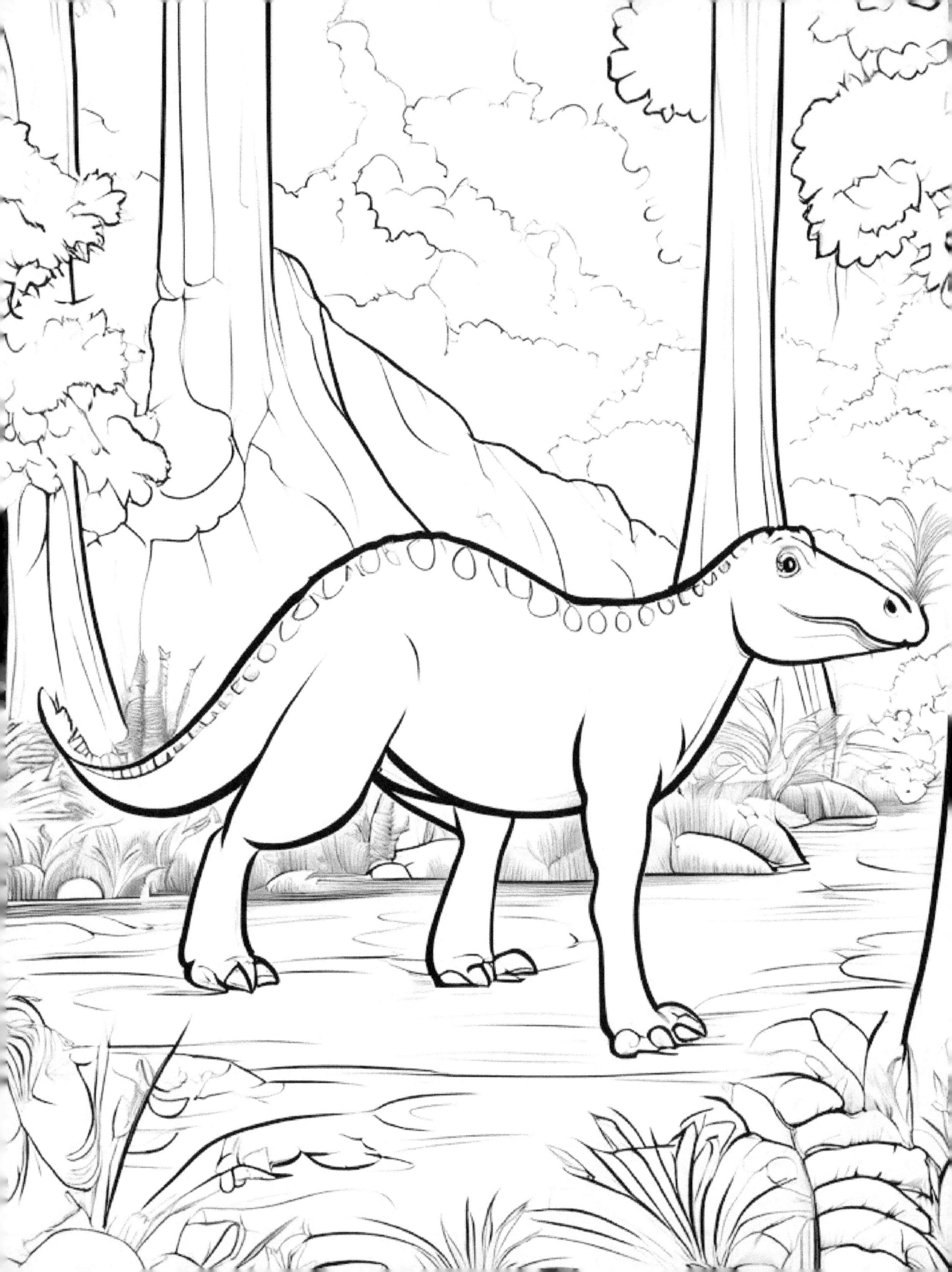

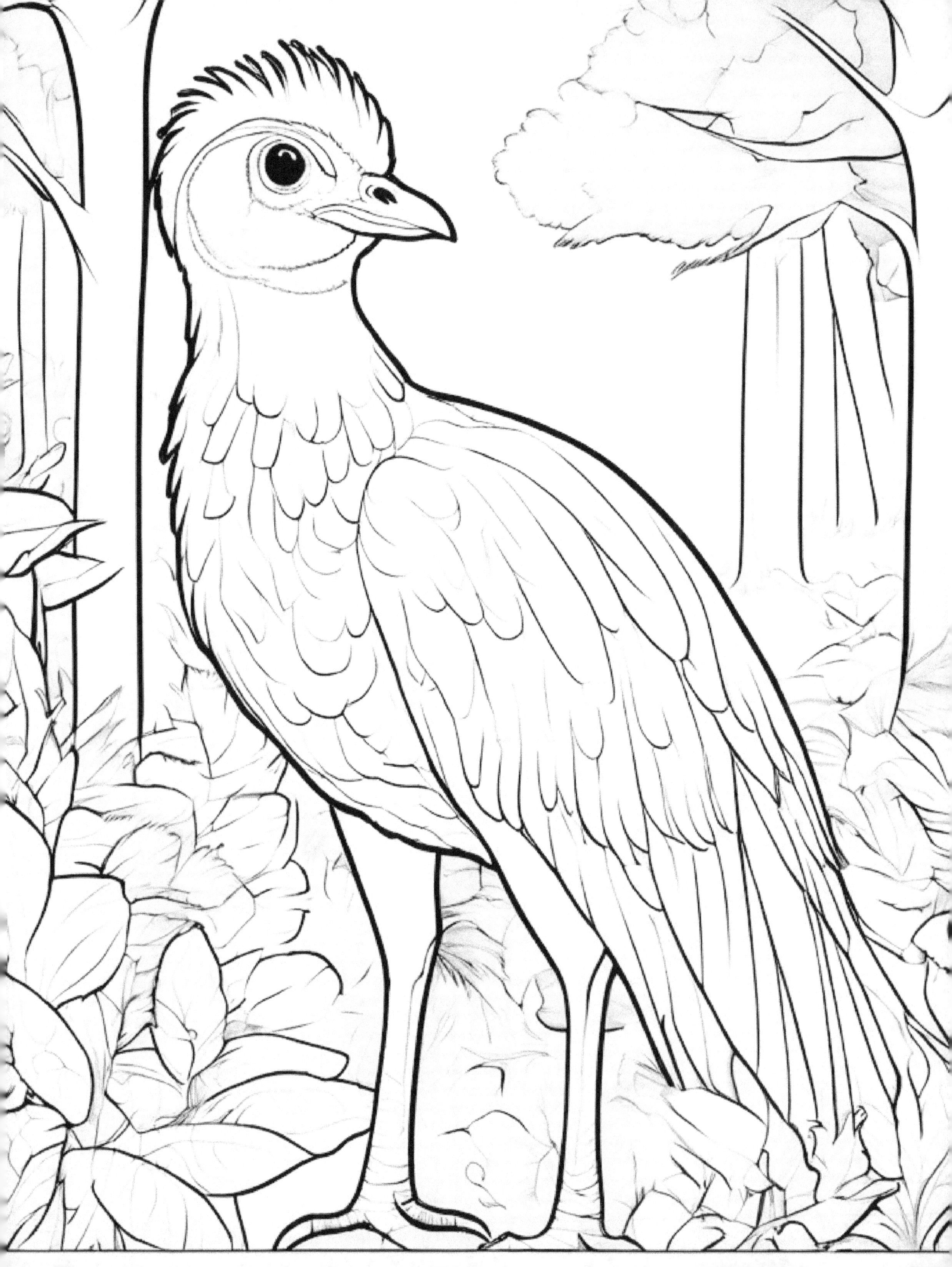

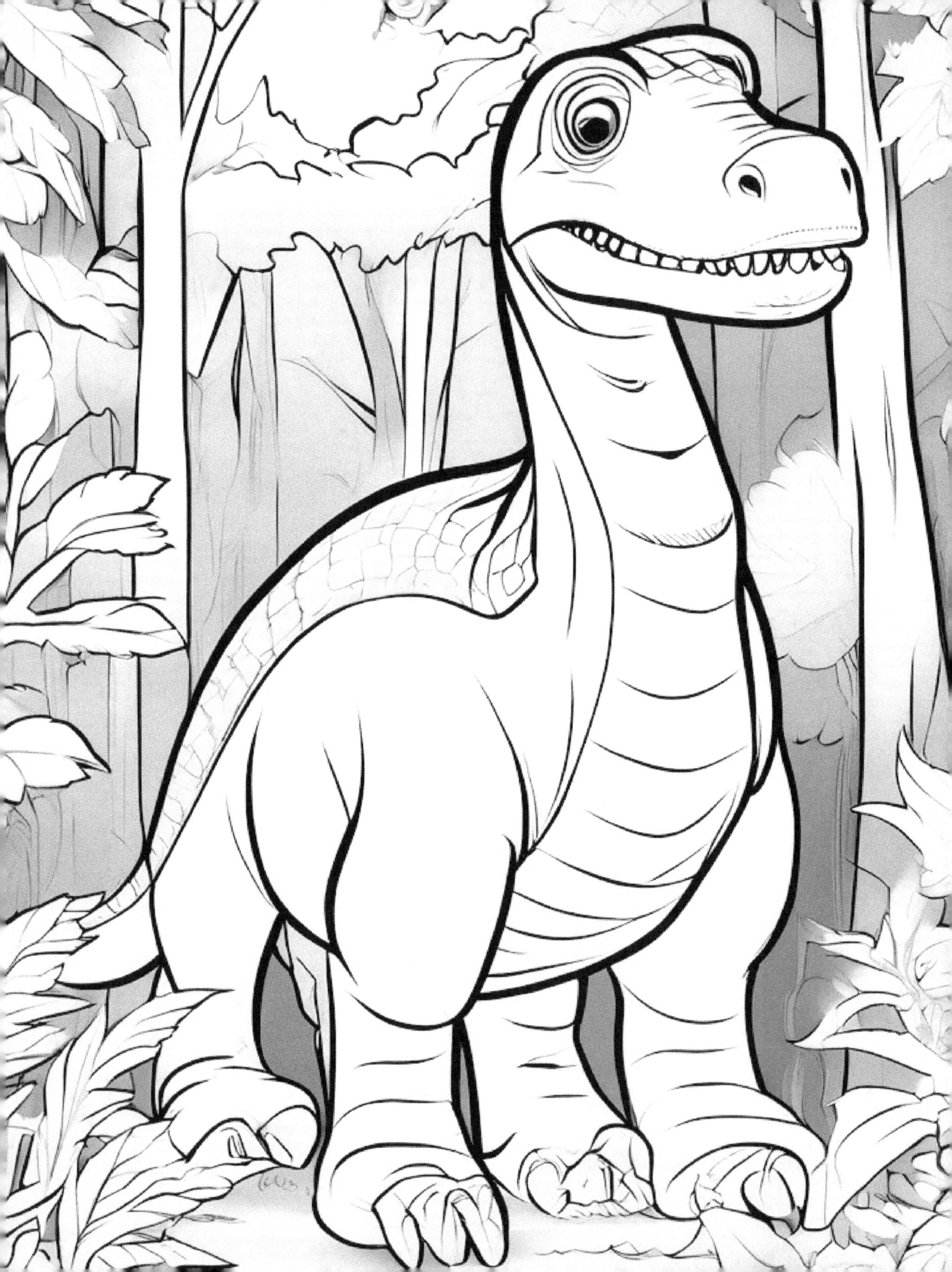

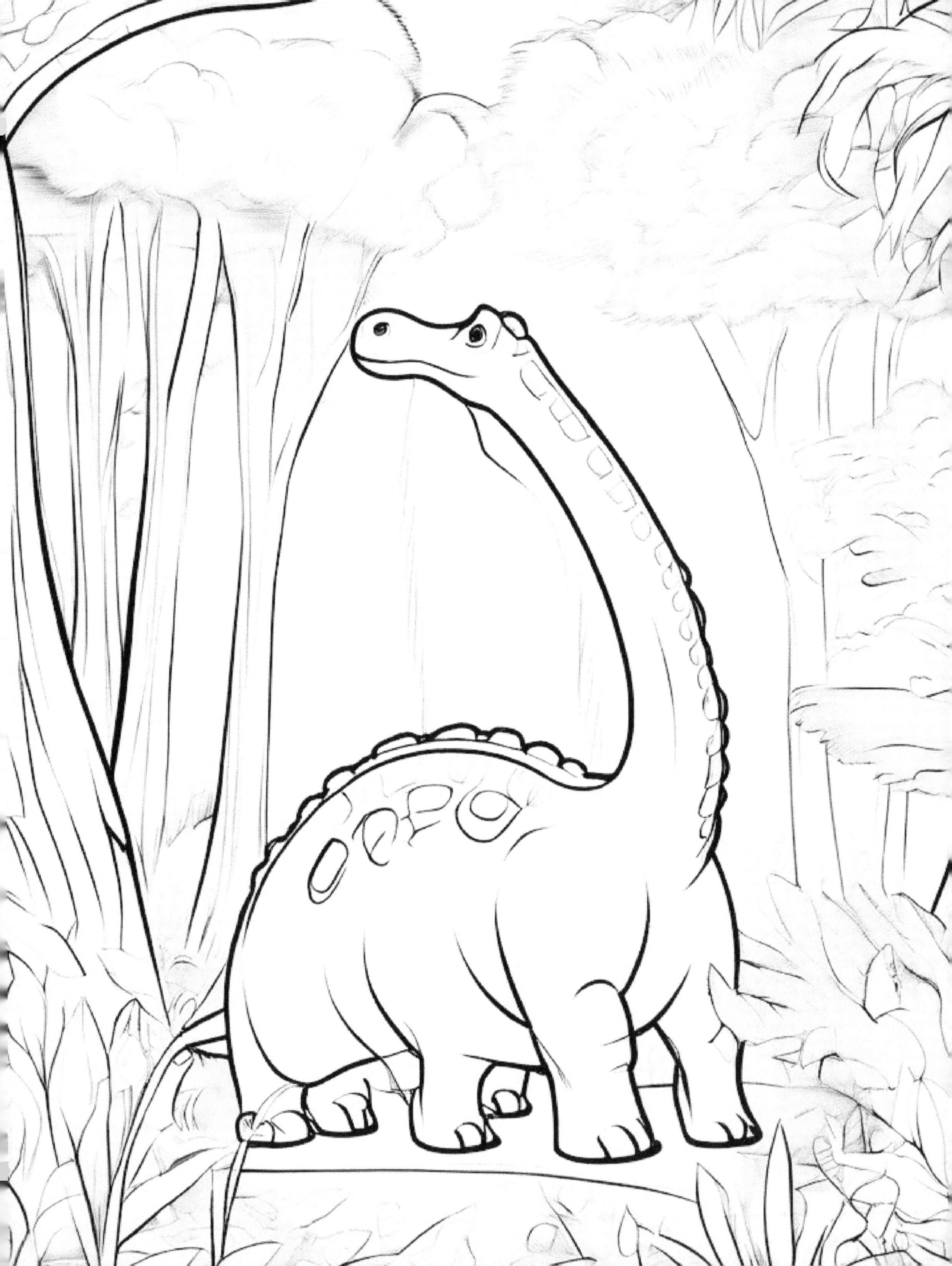

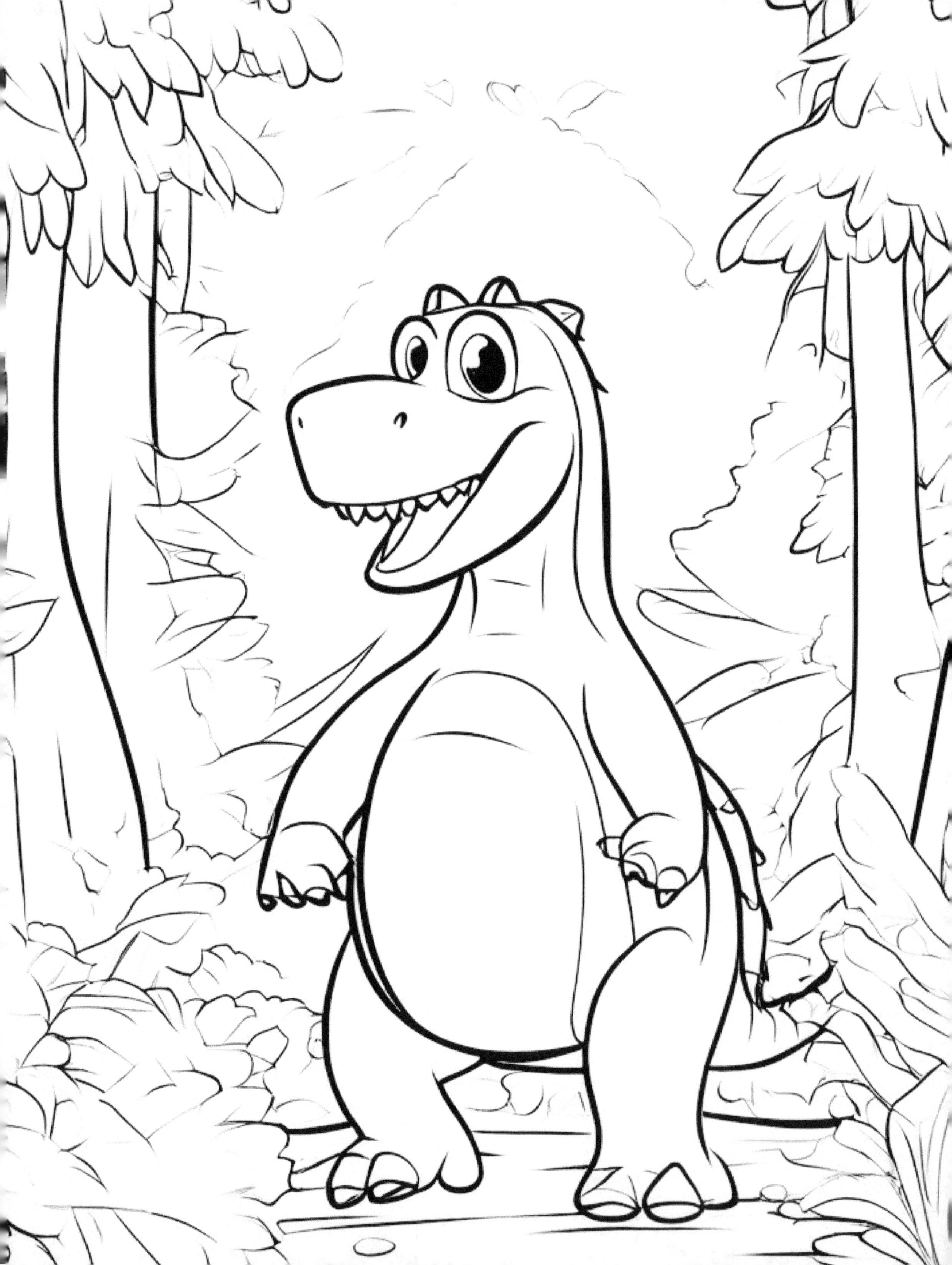

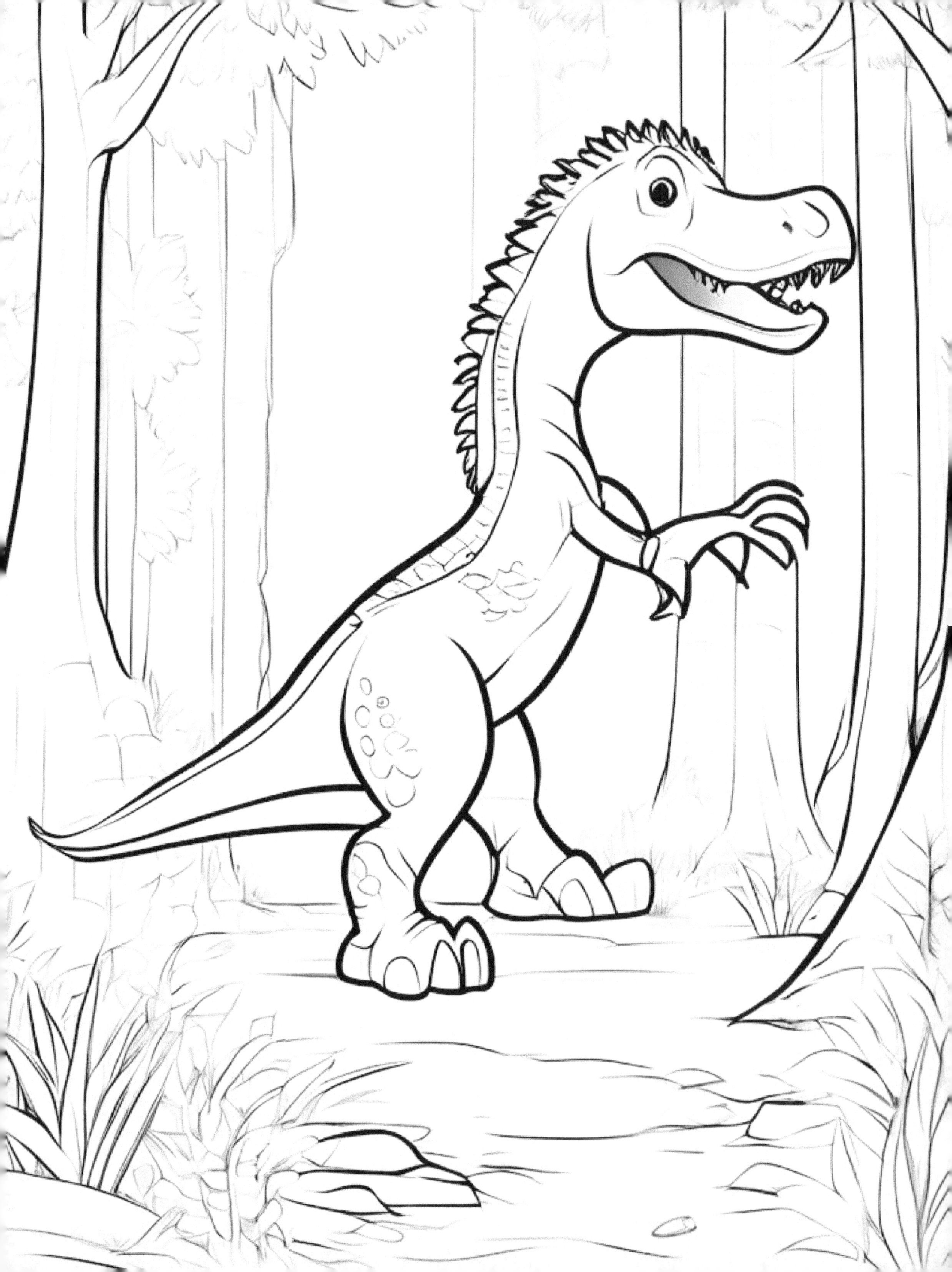

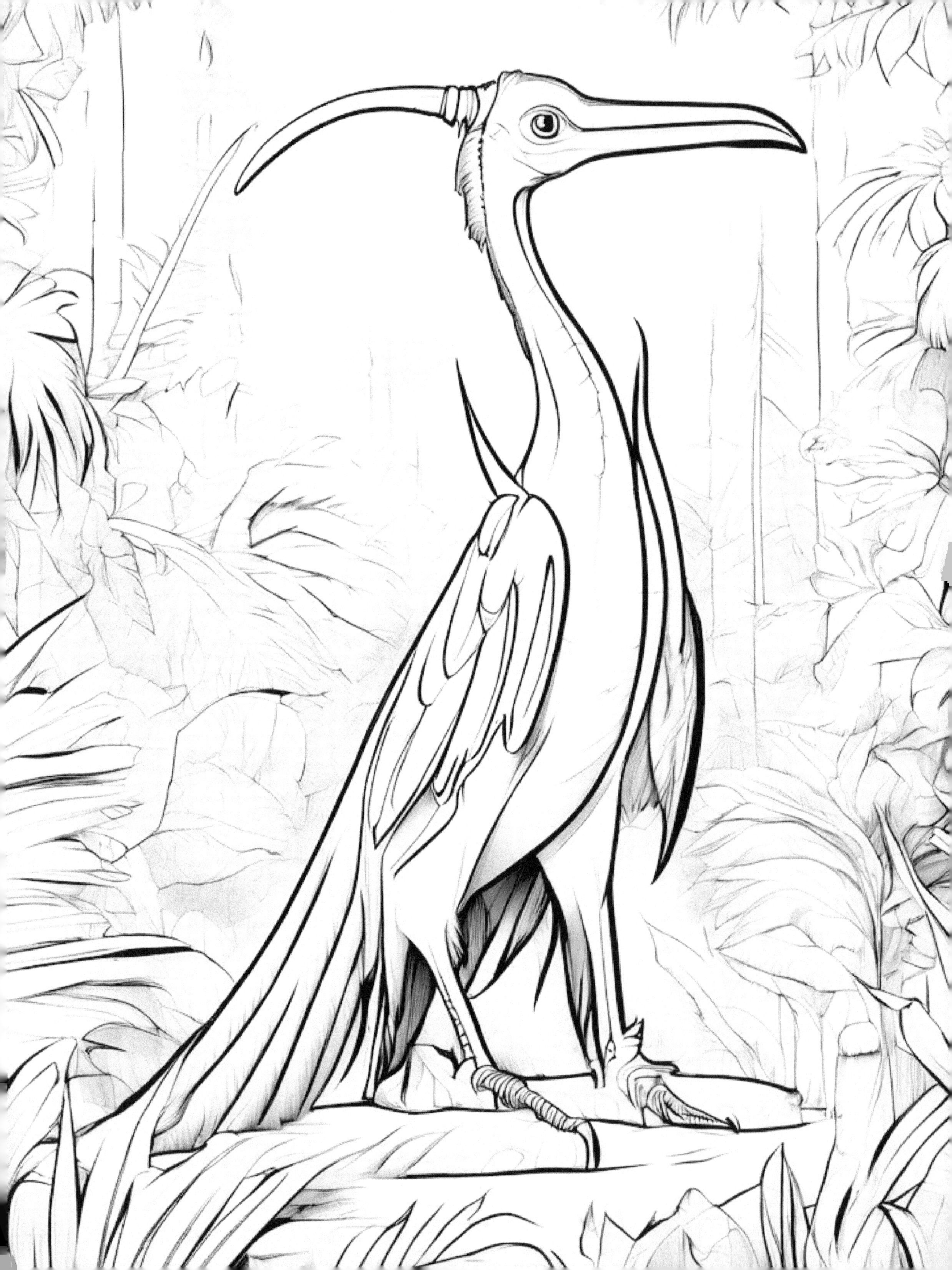

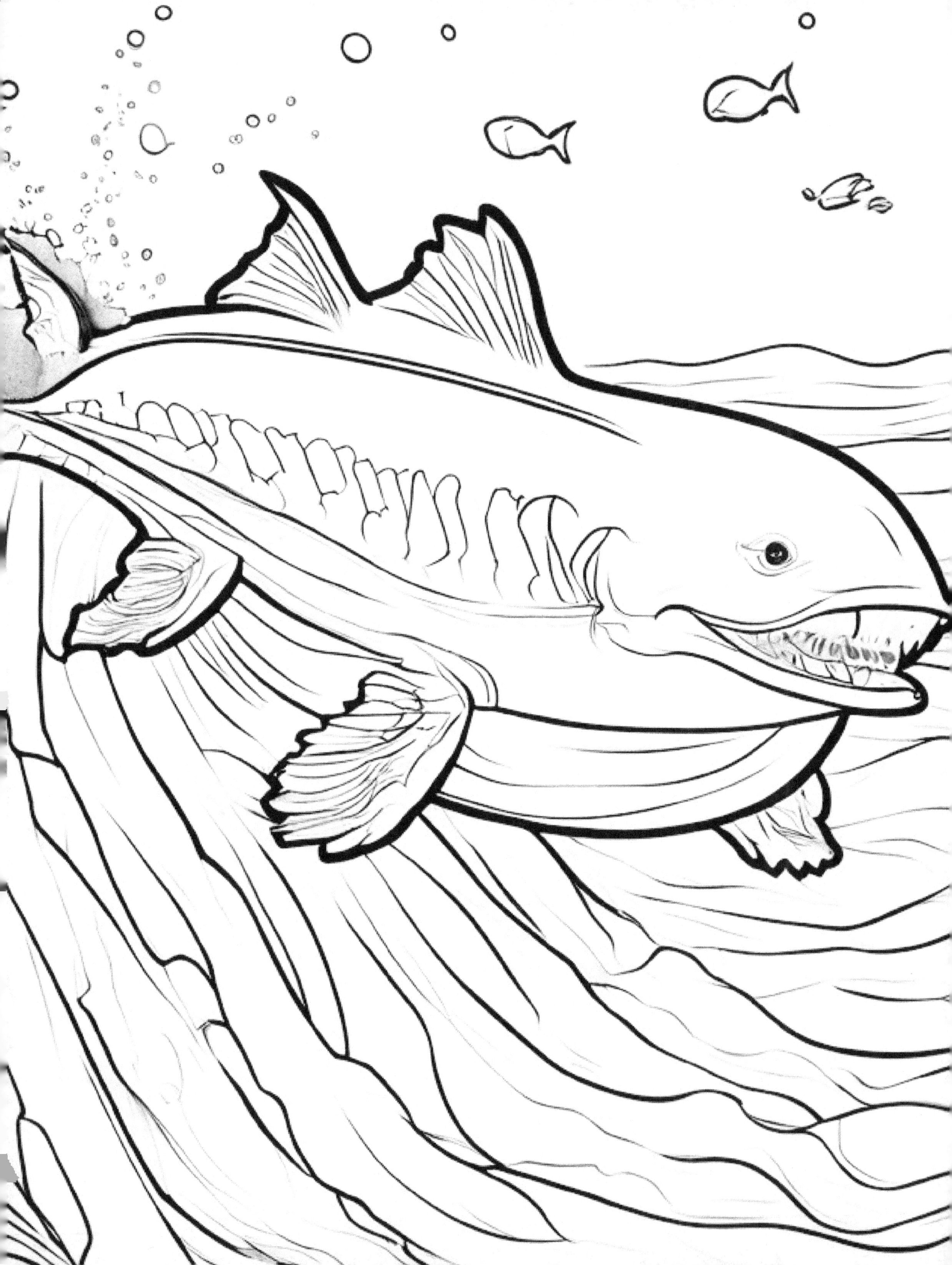

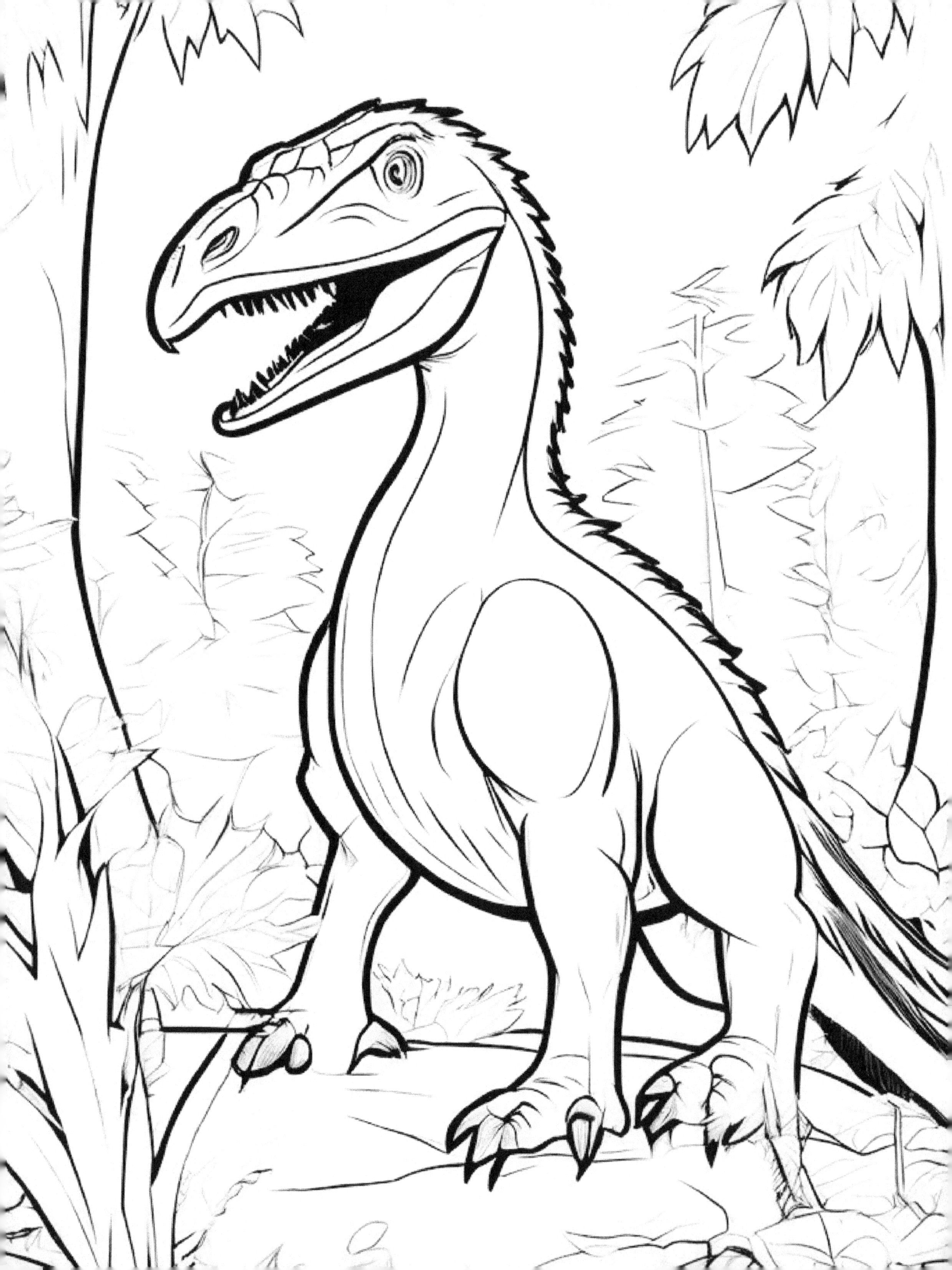

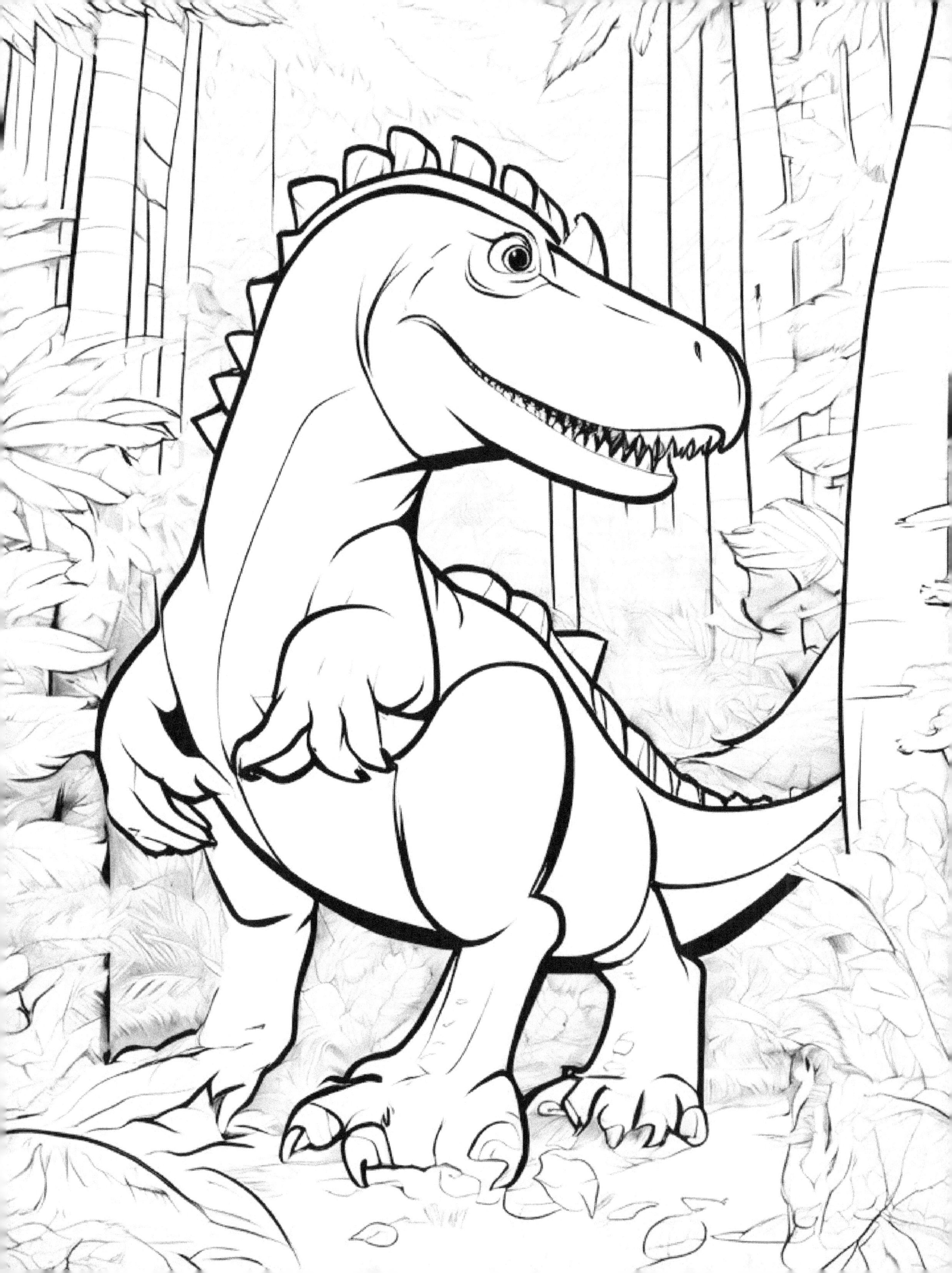

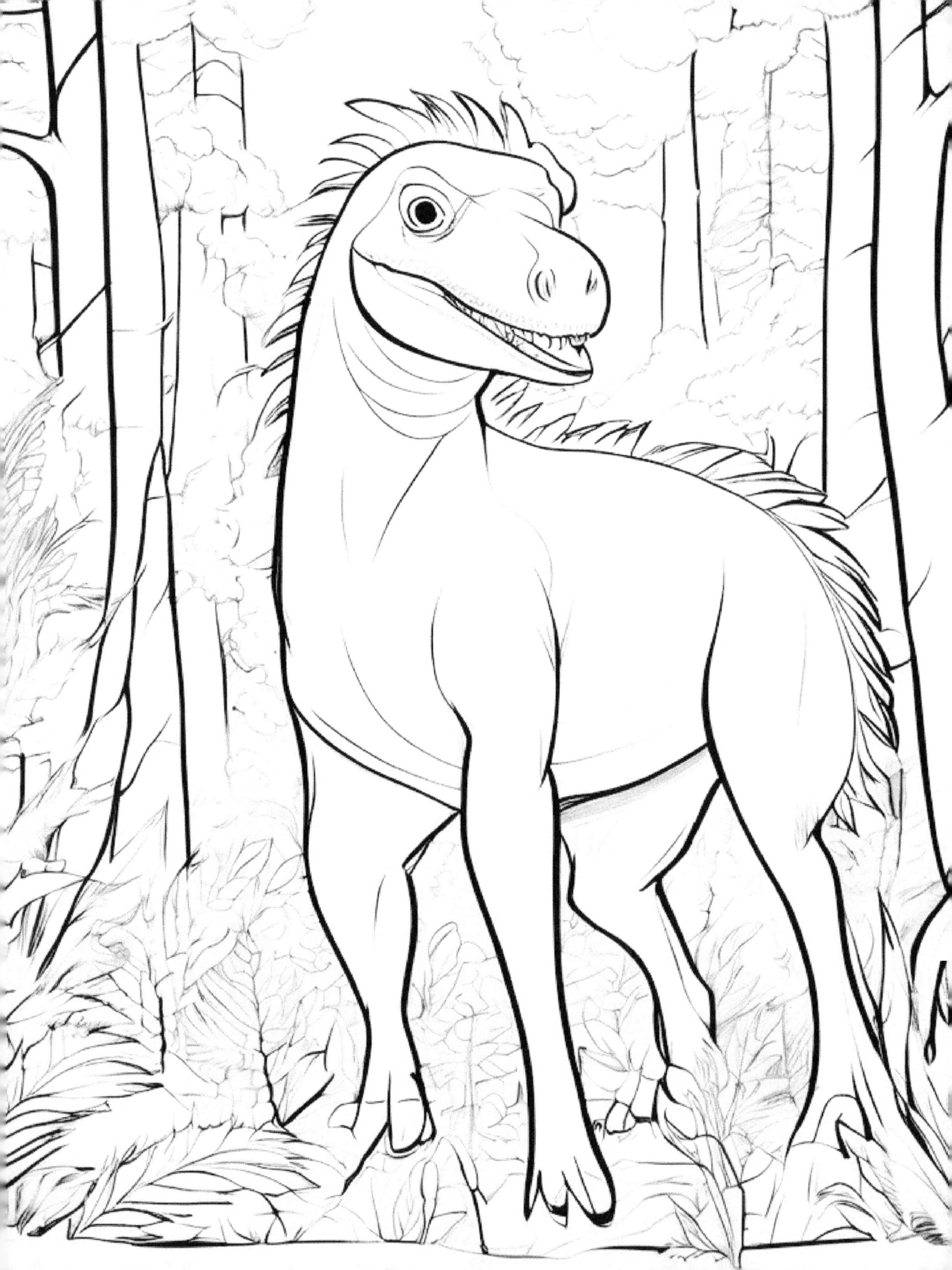

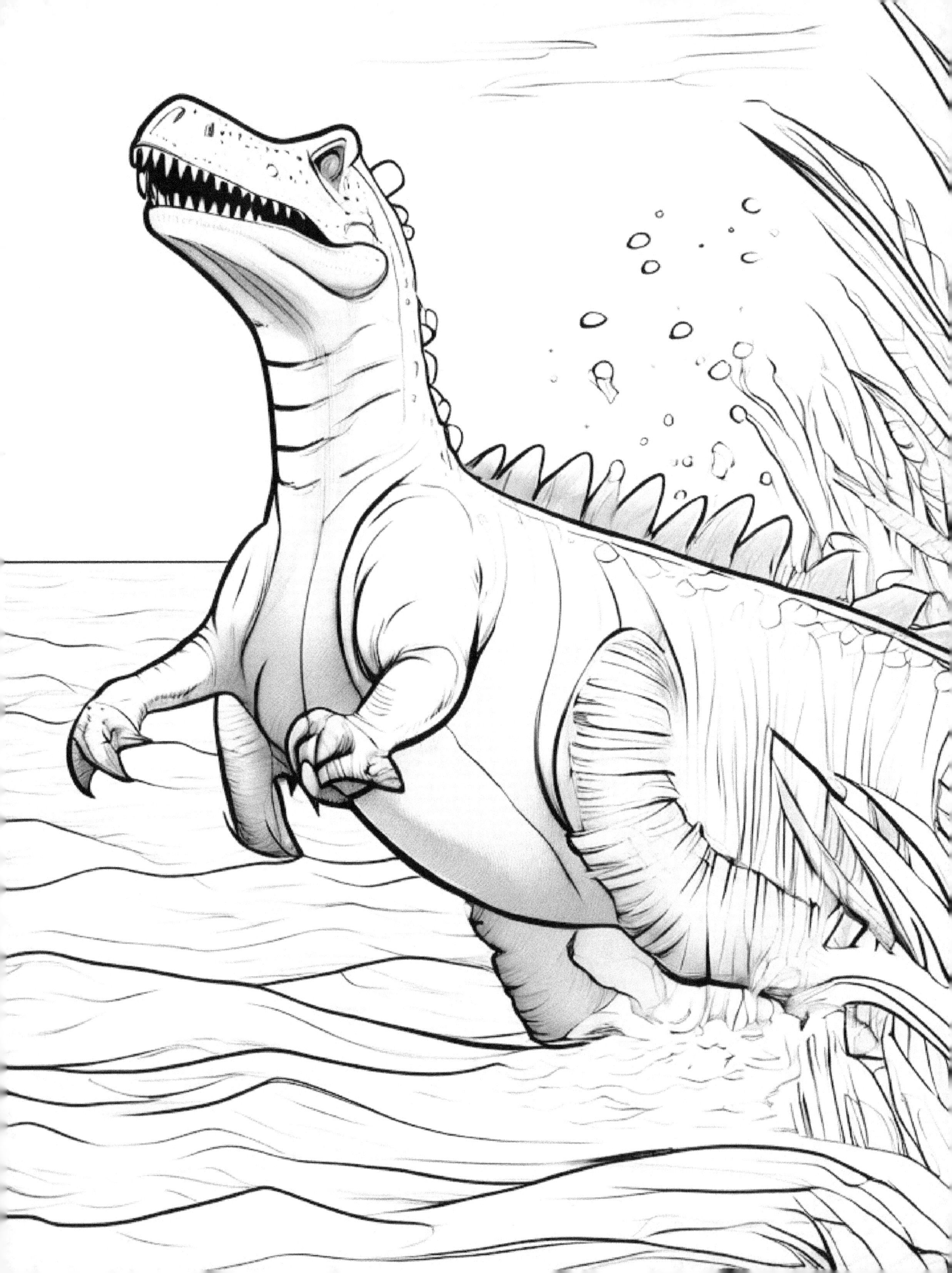

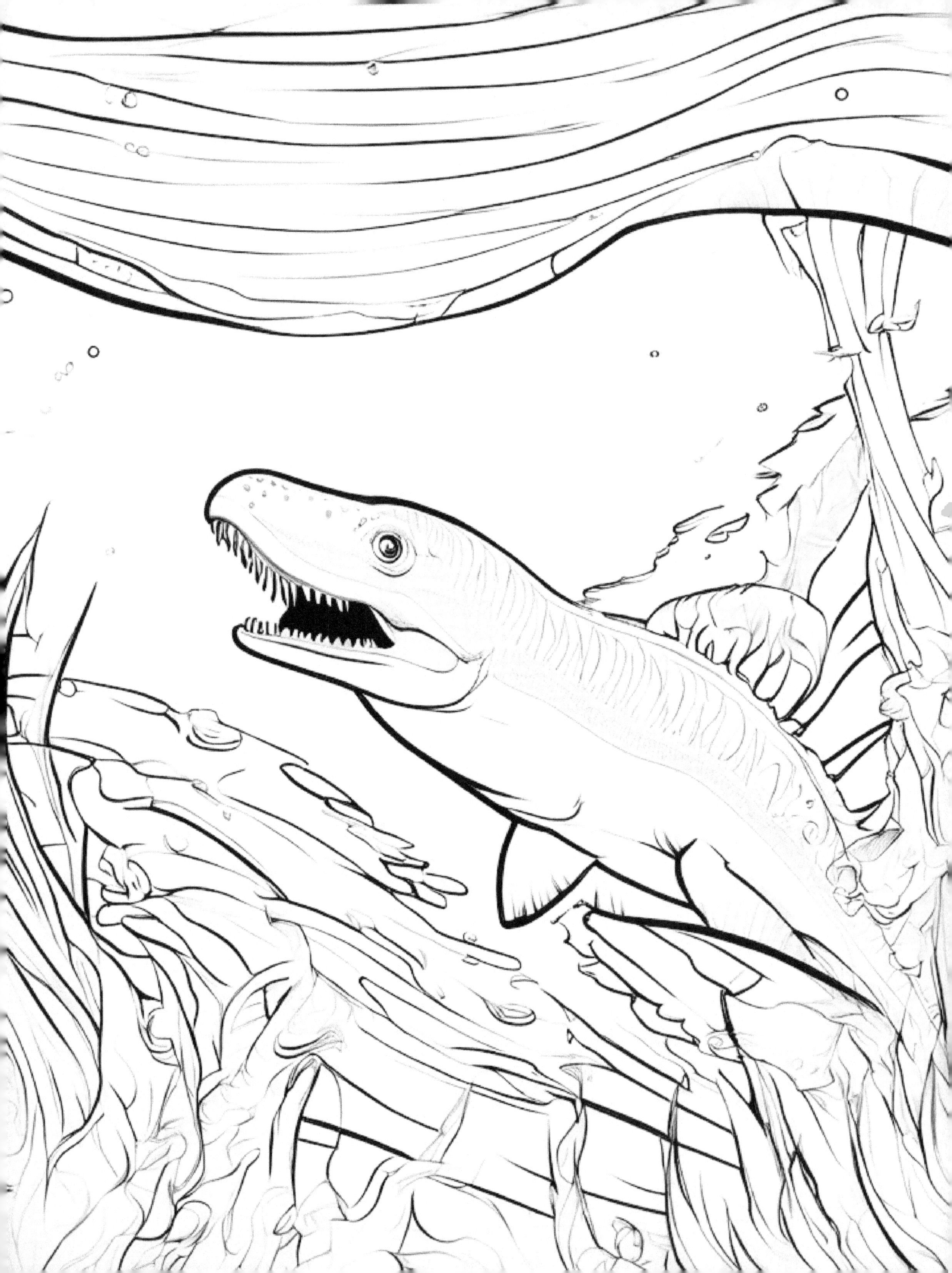

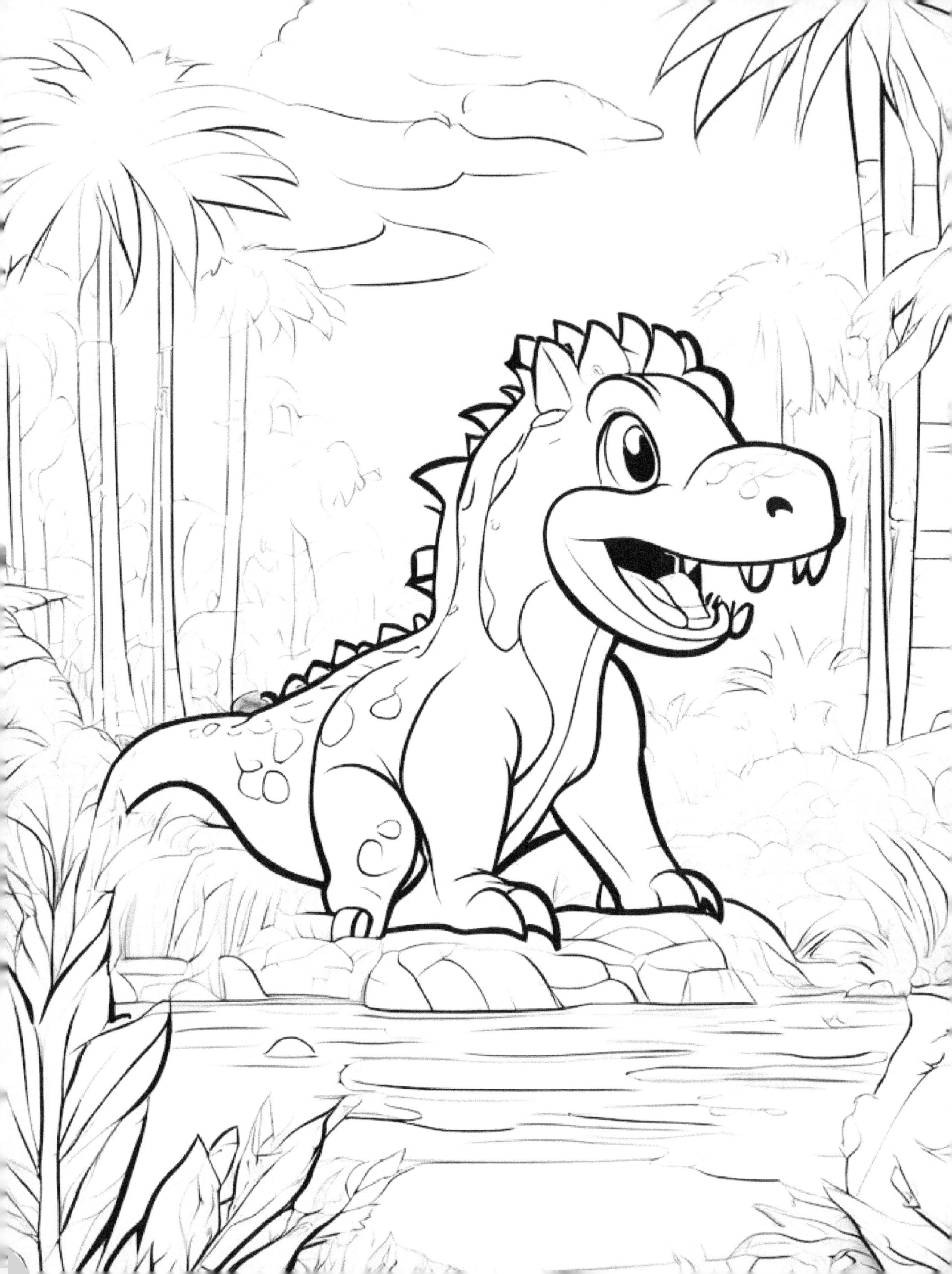

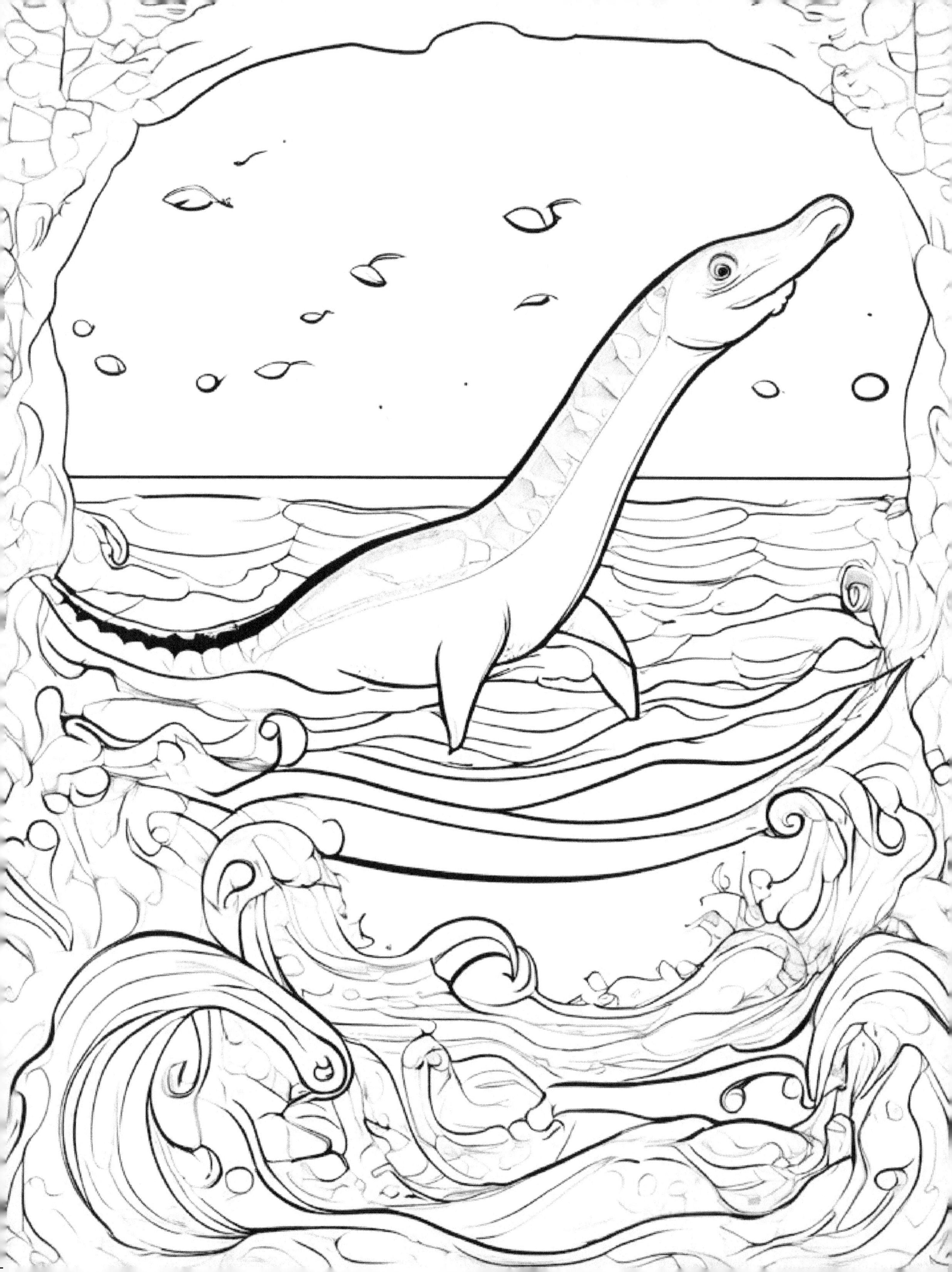

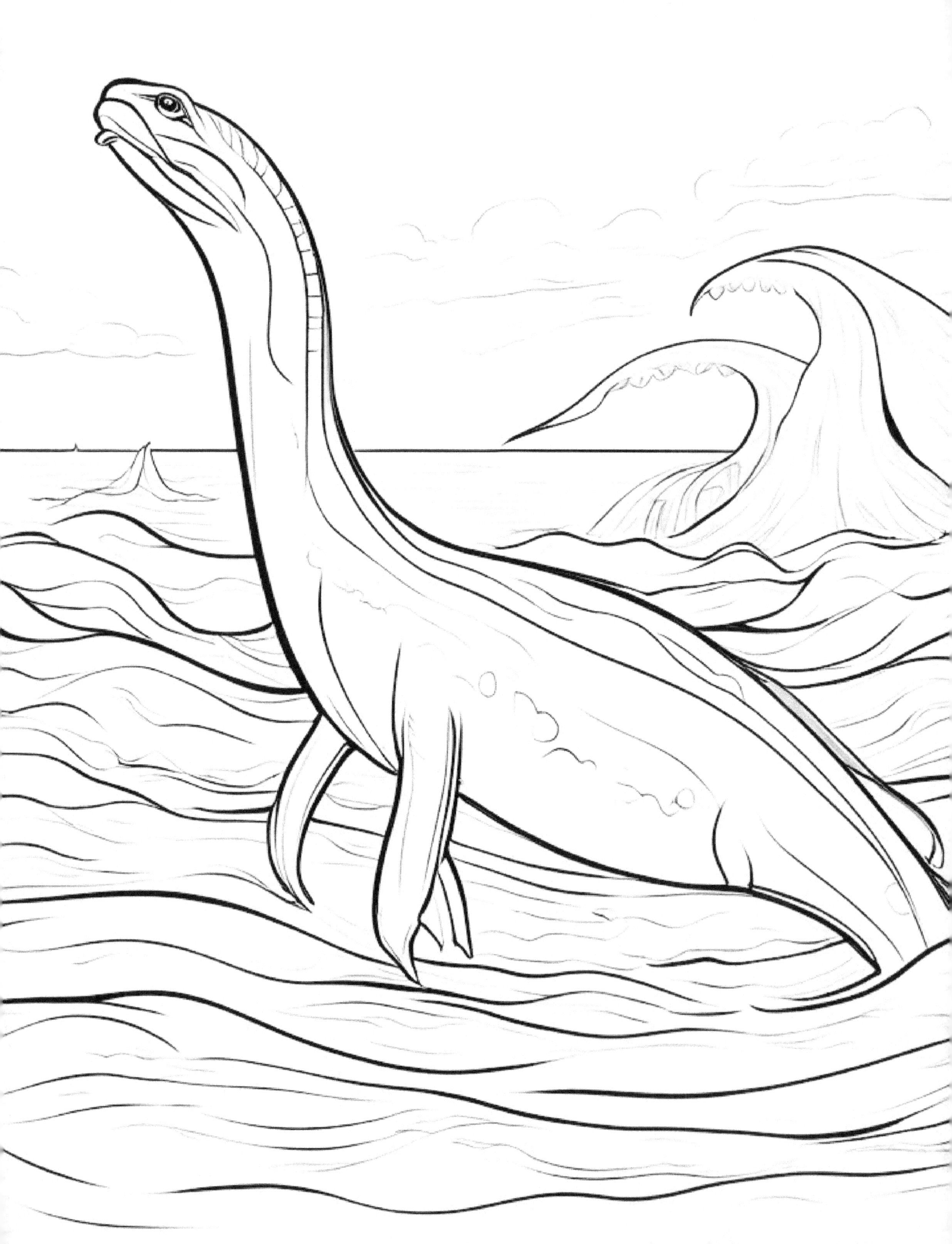